Edited by Sarah Graves and Angela Maher

Developing Graduate Employability

Case Studies in Hospitality, Leisure, Sport and Tourism

Threshold Press

First published 2008 by
Threshold Press Ltd
152 Craven Road
Newbury Berks RG14 5NR
Phone 01635-230272 and fax 01635-44804
email: publish@threshold-press.co.uk
www.threshold-press.co.uk

British Library Cataloguing in Publication Data
A catalogue record for this book is available from the British Library
ISBN 978-1-903152-19-5

Printed in England by Biddles Ltd, Kings Lynn

Contents

Acknowledgements

This project is funded by the Higher Education Funding Council for England (HEFCE) and the Department for Employment and Learning (DEL) under the Fund for the Development of Teaching and Learning (FDTL).

The editors and publisher are grateful to the Higher Education Academy for permission to reproduce Yorke and Knight's 39 Aspects of employability (Chapter 5, Appendix 3) and their USEM model (Chapter 10, Figure 1).

Editors' note

Please note where levels 1, 2 and 3 are mentioned in the text these are equivalent to HE levels 4, 5 and 6.

Introduction

The Fund for the Development of Teaching and Learning (FDTL) is a largely unsung success of the English and Northern Irish higher education funding bodies. This publication stands as a testament to its achievements in addressing key issues in learning, teaching and assessment in higher education (HE), and in particular the important area of student employability. The FDTL programme was established in England and Northern Ireland in December 1995 to 'support projects aimed at stimulating developments in teaching and learning in higher education, and to encourage the dissemination of good practice across the sector.' In the fifth and final round of funding (FDTL5), the subject disciplines of hospitality, leisure, sport and tourism (HLST) were invited to bid for up to £250,000 to support development projects designed to enhance student learning. Oxford Brookes and Sheffield Hallam Universities together successfully bid for maximum funding to support a three-year project *Enhancing Graduate Employability: embedding employability skills development in the curriculum* which started in October 2004 and involved ten institutional partners, spanning across the HLST subject areas.

The project, directed from Oxford Brookes, developed alongside the consultation process for, and publication of, the Leitch Review of Skills *Prosperity for all in the global economy – world class skills* (2006) and the subsequent strategy document *Higher Education at Work – High Skills: High Value* (2008). The latter consultation document sets ambitious targets in response to Lord Leitch's analysis of UK skills needs to 2020 and emphasises the point that:

> We want to see all universities treating student employability as a core part of their mission. So we believe it is reasonable to expect universities to take responsibility for how their students are prepared for the world of work.

The document also reiterates that:

> Employers particularly value broad 'employability' skills, such as communication, motivation, independence, analysis, confidence and problem solving. This is one of the strongest messages from employers to government.

Also, in October 2007 the Department for Innovation, Universities and Skills (DIUS) established a Student Listening Programme 'designed to amplify the student voice in Government' (DIUS, 2007). In early feedback from the new student juries, concern was expressed by students as to how much their courses increase their employability. Ministers undertaking the 'student listening visits' are being forcibly reminded that some students would like to have more experience of the world of work; develop a broader range of skills and have more variation in how they are assessed.

Looking beyond the UK, a key goal of the Bologna Process is to 'create a European space for higher education in order to enhance the employability and mobility of citizens' (CRE, 2005: 4). Bologna is having an impact on the shape of developments in HE beyond European boundaries and in Australia, the USA and South America, the link between education and employment would appear stronger than ever before.

In the light of these national and international developments in employability this project, and the valuable learning and teaching resources it has produced (see http://www.enhancingemployability.org.uk), is a particularly timely initiative.

The *Enhancing Graduate Employability* project

Although there is consensus amongst key stakeholders on the importance of addressing employability within HE, there remains some debate on how best this can be achieved, and indeed the extent to which HE can influence this aspect of student development. In an extensive review of educational provision Little concludes that:

> while there is international concern that higher education should enhance graduate employability, there is little evidence of systematic thinking about how best to do it, let alone any model that can be badged as 'best practice' and adopted wholesale. (2004: 4)

Within the context of hospitality, leisure, sport and tourism, employability has particular relevance because of the diversity of industries and the volatility of employment within these sectors. This means students in these disciplines often face particular challenges in gaining graduate jobs.

The project which forms the basis of this book is one response to the employability agenda by academics in HLST and the case studies provide practical examples of how employability can be embedded into these curricula. Each chapter describes the experiences of a different HE institution, and collectively the ten case studies reflect the rich variety of approaches that can be adopted in curriculum development for employability.

Approaches to embedding employability

Knight and Yorke, in *Learning, Curriculum and Employability in Higher Education* (2004) outline four main strategies currently in use within higher education for embedding employability in the curriculum. These include:

❏ embedding employability through the whole curriculum
❏ embedding employability in the core curriculum
❏ incorporating employability-related modules within the curriculum
❏ work-based or work-related learning within or in parallel with the curriculum.

Embedding employability through the whole curriculum

Employability through the whole curriculum is perhaps the most ambitious strategy in which a set of transferable skills or competencies are integrated through an entire programme. Within the context of the Enhancing Graduate Employability project, one case study in particular focuses explicitly on the relationship between PDP and employability (although other case studies also touch on this).

As outlined in chapter three, students studying sport at the University of Ulster are being asked to use the university's PDP system to help them audit and assess their employability skills and to identify 'gaps' in their skills base. This information is being used by students, in discussion with course tutors, to help them action plan for how they might enhance and develop their skills during an (optional) placement year or in their final year of study. This offers a useful example of how employability learning can be linked to wider institutional agendas such as PDP, and to current debates on how student achievement is measured and recorded (for example see Burgess Group Final Report published by Universities UK in 2007).

Embedding employability in the core curriculum

Embedding employability through the core curriculum involves the identification of a finite number of modules in which the development of a set of 'transferable' skills is addressed. This approach is arguably easier to implement than employability through the whole curriculum, particularly within large, diverse institutions and those that offer flexible modular programmes.

Several case studies contained in this book explore this approach and chapter four in particular emphasises this. The Department of Leisure, Tourism and Hospitality at the University of Gloucestershire have carefully explored the impact of embedding employability in the core curriculum. Having identified the skills of reflection and reflective writing as being important in the context of employability and personal development, the department has embedded activities into their core level 1, 2 and 3 modules to progressively foster student development.

Of particular note is the use of the technique of storytelling (Danto, 1985; McDury and Alterio, 2003) at level 3 to encourage deeper reflection on, and to help students make sense of, the complex experiences that occur during their work placement. Other activities include the completion of a personal skills audit and authoring of a reflective portfolio, in addition to the use of critical narrative post-placement.

Incorporating employability-related modules within the curriculum

A further approach to embedding employability involves the development of specific employability-related modules such as personal skills development and career planning. This again may represent a more practical approach to embedding employability skills development and is a popular method within the HE sector. The case study undertaken by Sheffield Hallam University contained at chapter seven involves the piloting of a module entitled *Developing Your Management Skills*. This module is aimed at postgraduate hospitality and tourism students and designed to help them develop career management skills, drawing explicitly on students' part-time work experiences which the researchers have identified as an increasingly common aspect of studying at the University. At Oxford Brookes University employability is being embedded via a compulsory first-year module in which skills are evaluated and assessed using, amongst other techniques, a card-sort exercise that focuses attention on what employers want and what makes employees successful at work.

Work-based or work-related learning modules within the curriculum

Work-based learning (WBL) and work-related learning (WRL) are strategies most commonly associated with enhancing employability: several case studies drawn together in this book illustrate this. The research being conducted at Liverpool John Moores University has focused on establishing a WBL forum made up of employers, lecturers and students that draw together the views of these key stakeholders 'to produce a curriculum structure that transfers students' employability potential into reality'. The partnership aspect of this case study is critical to developing a curriculum that is effective in developing 'highly employable graduates'. City College Norwich and Westminster Kingsway College case studies also research aspects of employer engagement as a means of enhancing students' employability, whereas case studies being undertaken at Leeds Metropolitan and the University of Worcester focus on postgraduate work placement and entrepreneurship respectively.

Conclusion

Higher Education institutions in the UK, working with employer partners, are learning that 'vocational' courses do not necessarily automatically produce employable graduates, and an increasing number have graduate employability prominent in their mission statements. The case studies contained in this book should further encourage that development by providing evidence-based examples of curriculum interventions that work, and by providing access to teaching and learning resources that enable students to develop competencies for employment.

Val Butcher

July 2008

References

CRE (2005) *Defining Employability*. Sheffield: Centre for Research and Evaluation Sheffield Hallam University. Available at http://www.shu.ac.uk/research/cre/Employabilitydefiningemployability.htm

Danto, A. C. (1985) *Narration and Knowledge*. New York: Columbia University Press

DIUS (2007). *Student Listening Programme.* Available at http://www.dius.gov.uk/policy/he_slp.html

DIUS (2008). *Higher Education at Work: High Skills: High Value*. Available at www.dius.gov.uk/consultations/con_0408_hlss.html

Leitch Review of Skills (2006) *Prosperity for All in the Global Economy – World Class Skills*. London: HM Treasury. Available at http://www.hm-treasury.gov.uk/media/6/4/leitch_finalreport051206.pdf

Knight, P. and Yorke, M. (2004). *Learning, Curriculum and Employability in Higher Education*. London: RoutledgeFalmer

Little, B. (2004). Employability and work-based learning. *Learning and Employability Series One*. ESECT: The Higher Education Academy

McDury, J. and Alterio, M. (2003). *Learning through Storytelling in Higher Education: Using Reflection and Experience to Improve Learning*. London: Kogan Page

Universities UK (2007) *Beyond the Honours Degree Classification: Burgess Group Final Report*. Available at .http://bookshop.universitiesuk.ac.uk/downloads/Burgess_final.pdf

About the authors

Ian Beattie is a Senior Lecturer in Sport Development at Liverpool John Moores University and teaches on a range of courses within the Centre for Sport, Dance and Outdoor Education.

Karen Bill has recently left the University of Worcester, where she was Principal Lecturer in Enterprise and Knowledge Transfer Fellow, to become Associate Dean in the School of Sport, Performing Arts and Leisure at the University of Wolverhampton.

Deirdre Brennan is a Senior Lecturer in the School of Sports Studies at the University of Ulster at Jordanstown who specialises in physical education.

John Buswell is Principal Lecturer in the Department of Leisure, Tourism and Hospitality Management at the University of Gloucestershire and, for the last three years, Director of the phase 5 FDTL Project META: From PDP to CPD. He is also liaison officer for Leisure for the HE Academy Subject Centre for Hospitality, Leisure, Sport and Tourism, based at Oxford Brookes University.

Val Butcher was Senior Adviser for Employability with the Higher Education Academy until July 2007 and a consultant to higher education in matters relating to employability in the academic curriculum throughout the UK and Europe. She is continuing her consultancy role in her 'retirement'. She was a Fellow of NICEC (the National Institute of Careers Education and Counselling) 1995–2005 and is now a NICEC Associate and is currently a Visiting Fellow at the Centre for Employability in the Humanities (Centre of Excellence) at the University of Central Lancashire.

Sarah Graves is a Lecturer in the Department of Hospitality, Leisure and Tourism Management at Oxford Brookes University Business School. Sarah has been Project Manager for the FDTL5 *Enhancing Graduate Employability* project since 2005 and, in addition to managing the network of ten institutional partners, has organised related national and regional events. Sarah is currently undertaking doctoral research exploring the career progression of graduates from non-traditional backgrounds.

Vicki Hingley, Lecturer at City College Norwich, is course director of BA(Hons) Hospitality, Tourism and Leisure Management and course tutor on Hospitality and Tourism pathway Foundation degrees.

Stephanie Jameson is Principal Lecturer for Assessment, Learning and Teaching in the Leslie Silver International Faculty at Leeds Metropolitan University.

Angela Maher is a Principal Lecturer in the Department of Hospitality, Leisure and Tourism Management at Oxford Brookes University Business School where she also has responsibility for graduate careers and work experience programmes. Angela has directed the FDTL5 *Enhancing Graduate Employability* project since 2004.

Marie Murphy is Head of the School of Sports Studies and Co-director of the Ulster Sports Academy at the University of Ulster. She is a BASES-accredited exercise scientist and a fellow of both the Higher Education Authority and the American College of Sports Medicine.

Emma Martin is Principal Lecturer in Human Resource Management based in the Hospitality subject team at Sheffield Hallam University. She is currently the post-graduate programme leader for Tourism, Hospitality, Events and Food.

Scott McCabe is Lecturer in Tourism Management and Marketing at the Christel DeHaan Tourism and Travel Research Institute of Nottingham University Business School. He is the author of a number of journal articles and book chapters on these subjects and the forthcoming book *Marketing Communications in Tourism and Hospitality: Concepts, Strategies and Cases.*

Sarah Nixon is a Principal Lecturer at Liverpool John Moores University and the leader of the Centre for Excellence in Teaching and Learning (CETL) for the Faculty of Education, Community and Leisure.

Bob Snape is a Reader in the School of Health and Social Sciences at the University of Bolton.

Angela Tomkins is a Senior Lecturer in the Department of Leisure, Tourism and Hospitality Management at the University of Gloucestershire. Angela's interests concern lifelong learning, the role of the 'reflective practitioner' and the importance of professional development.

Cath Walker is the Curriculum Leader for the Sport Development with PE programme at Liverpool John Moores University and teaches on a range of courses within the Centre for Sport, Dance and Outdoor Education.

Linda Waghorn is a full-time Lecturer at Westminster Kingsway College in the School of Hospitality, Leisure and Tourism where she was involved in the introduction of Foundation degrees into their higher education programme. Her principal areas of teaching are organisational behaviour and research methods.

Charles Whittaker is a Senior Lecturer in Hospitality and Director of MBA Programmes for the Department of Hospitality, Leisure and Tourism Management at Oxford Brookes University. He is a chartered accountant and held senior finance posts with major hotel companies for many years before turning to teaching.

From potential to achievement: enhancing students' value to employers

Ian Beattie, Sarah Nixon and Cath Walker
Liverpool John Moores University

This case study uses stakeholder feedback on the value of work-based learning to improve student induction procedures for work placement

This case study sets out to develop core requirements in relation to the employability agenda within a BA (Hons) Sport Development with Physical Education (PE) programme at Liverpool John Moores University. This was achieved through examining employability perceptions of employers, students and work-based learning (WBL) partners. The focus for the intervention was on Level 2 and 3 undergraduate students, approximately 80 in each year, with the intention of supporting progression and development of students through these two levels on the road to becoming employable graduates.

Student feedback on employability and WBL was gathered both before and after placement at Level 2 to explore views about employability issues, understanding of employability and to gain insight into the substance of their work experiences. From the resulting data for academic year 2005–06, the student induction processes for WBL at both Levels 2 and 3 was amended and enhanced in relation to the findings. Student focus groups and data from an employer questionnaire also informed decision-making.

Evaluation activities identified 89% of students expressing the view that WBL is important. Additionally, developing knowledge, skills and experience for employability was seen as very important or important by students because of the expectations of potential employers. The focus groups highlighted the view that WBL aspects of the course had enhanced students' experience, skills and knowledge in relation to employability. Moreover post-WBL, the students believed that their degree as a whole had positively impacted upon their employability. The data revealed that 69% felt it was enabling them to develop their employability skills, 70% that it was developing their knowledge and 69% believed the degree was enabling them to develop relevant experience.

Work was also undertaken with employers, with the establishment and continued development of a Work-Based Learning Management Group proving an immensely positive outcome of the case study.

Objectives

The objectives of the case study are:

1   To examine employer views/opinions on graduate employability skills they require.
2   To develop a work-based learning discussion forum involving all stakeholders.
3   To examine the views and opinions of students related to work-based learning and employability.
4   To disseminate findings of the case study to inform our own and our partners' professional practice.
5   To establish a programme of career development seminars to enhance students' employability.

Context/rationale

The work undertaken within this case study has been focused on one programme, the BA (Hons) Sport Development with PE degree, at Liverpool John Moores University (LJMU). Employability is currently high on the agenda within LJMU. Within university policy there is acknowledgement that the higher education learning environment is concerned with the development of students' knowledge, skills and understanding and the university's goal is to become the UK university whose graduates are most valued by employers. LJMU's strategic approach is to encourage and enable all students to develop, alongside their academic achievements, the generic skills that employers demand and value (LJMU, 2006).

In 2005 the university was successfully awarded a Centre for Excellence in Teaching and Learning (CETL) and the team who have worked on this case study are a part of this structure and related initiatives. Both the CETL and the university focus have enhanced the work of the project due to the input of extra resources, knowledge and experiences.

Employability has always been an integral component of work undertaken by sport staff in the Centre for Sport, Dance and Outdoor Education, but it was felt that this needed to be enhanced and developed to ensure that our graduates were well placed to go out into their respective fields and have the ability to be successful.

In a national context, sport and recreation had a workforce of 363,100 people in paid employment in 2004, working in 25,000 businesses and organisations throughout the UK. Economic forecasts indicate that the sector has the potential to expand to a workforce of 442,500 in paid employment by 2012 (SkillsActive, 2006). It is imperative therefore that graduates are given the skills needed to compete in this industry.

With the university and national agendas in mind, the project set out to examine and develop the core requirements in relation to the employability agenda within the Sport Development programme. This information was then used to enhance the curriculum to better prepare students entering the employment market, and also to enhance tutor knowledge about employability. This aim was to be achieved through examining perceptions and views from employers, from students and from work-based learning partners. The focus was on Level 2 and 3 students, approximately 80 in each year, and the progression and development of students through these two levels to graduation. A core group of three staff from within the teaching team, who are primarily responsible for the curriculum and work-based leaning, delivered the project and shared the findings as they progressed with the rest of the programme team.

This work has centred strongly on the student experience itself, with perhaps less emphasis placed on linking theory and practice. This said, the conceptual work of Yorke and Knight (2006) has underpinned the changes adopted in the curriculum. The project team adopted Yorke and Knight's definition of employability and used this to inform their approach to developing the curriculum, and to support student development. Thus the definition of employability in this context is:

> a set of achievements – skills, understanding and personal attributes – that makes graduates more likely to gain employment and be successful in their chosen occupations, which benefits themselves, the workforce and the economy.

> (Yorke and Knight, 2006: 8)

According to Yorke and Knight (2006: 14) there are a 'spectrum of ways that employability can be developed through the curriculum.' The interventions within this case study have been based mainly around work-based learning, and specifically work placement (Harvey, Geall and Moon, 1998; Little et al, 2002; Little and ESECT colleagues, 2006). The team also supported the view of Blackwell et al (2001) who see the characteristics of quality WBL as: stakeholder understanding, induction and de-briefing of WBL, formative assessment, reflection and the use of a portfolio. Moon (2004) points out that rather than leaving the student unclear about what to learn during a work placement, institutions need to specify learning outcomes that focus the student's learning and encourage reflection about what they have learned. Harvey et al (1997) state that stronger links between employers and higher education have been seen as desirable. All of these elements were either developed or enhanced by the approaches taken within this study and are reflected in each of the case study objectives.

Description

The work that has taken place within this project has been primarily about informing the curriculum and ensuring, as much as possible, a best fit between the students' expected experiences and development through learning and the external employers' needs and requirements of a graduate in this field.

Student views on WBL were gained both before and after placement to assess what they thought and felt about their experiences and wider employability issues. A mixed method was used in relation to this data collection utilising both questionnaires and focus groups. The same questions were asked the following year to explore any change in views in relation to interventions mentioned later.

A number of tools were used to investigate employer needs in relation to sport graduates. A questionnaire was developed and distributed to a range of placement providers (approximately 150), to explore opinions and beliefs about the employability of graduates and what a university should be providing for its students. This information has been compared to the general sector skills data and other data from similar programmes within the faculty. The results show that employers seek similar traits in graduates and this information has been used to inform the presentation and delivery of employability-related topics in the curriculum.

A WBL Management Group was established to ensure that the programme and its links to the external environment where as strong as possible. This group consists of placement providers and key figures within sport and leisure in our region. Meetings take place twice a year and are facilitated by the programme WBL coordinator. The structure of the group enables the membership to examine the curriculum especially in relation to WBL and to feed into and help the programme team develop their curriculum appropriately. Action points from the meetings feed into the programme team and progress is reported back to the next management group meeting. This ensures a shared flow of information and actions developed. The employer members of this group also take students on placement and are able to feed into the programme any issues around supporting students. This has influenced curriculum practice in the following year. This approach has been evaluated by two focus groups, where members were asked about this method of curriculum enhancement and the benefits to both themselves and the students.

The student induction processes for WBL at both Levels 2 and 3 have been altered and enhanced in relation to the findings of both the employer questionnaire and focus groups. This enhancement has taken the form of an enhanced curriculum delivery relating to what employers look for in graduates and which skills are important. A number of methods were used, including showing the students the key data findings, bringing in employers from the WBL Management Group to talk through some of the issues, and using an interactive computer-based programme to help students independently work on skill awareness and development. Throughout Level 3 (academic year 2006–07), self-appraisal and analysis has been more tightly mapped into personal development processes (PDP) used in assessment. It is hoped that by doing this the students will have a greater understanding of employer needs, their own strengths and weaknesses in relation to this, and therefore be able to address any identified skill gaps.

The 2006–07 Level 3 students were also shown the findings from their focus groups at Level 2 and used this as a baseline to measure their own development and to look at where they need to go next. This has proved to be a particularly successful strategy as they really connected with their own data and were able to reflect back to what that experience was like and how they have developed since. This cohort also engaged in an on-line discussion forum while completing their WBL. They were able to interact both with the tutor and each other, and the findings to date indicate this has helped them to develop their awareness and confidence both in their own ability and their key skills development.

Evaluation

This evaluation provides a summary of findings on student perception pre- and post-WBL for academic year 2005–06 and pre-WBL for academic year 2006–07. A brief summary of employer perceptions is also provided, as well as the perceptions of members of the WBL Management Group. Detail of the blackboard discussion boards used to support students during placement is also provided.

Summary of student data for academic year 2005–06
❑ 89% thought WBL was important.
❑ 56% changed their opinion of career choices post-placement.
❑ The results found that 83% of the sample stated that they know what employability is, and after placement 93% said that WBL had increased this understanding.
Knowledge, skills and experience relating to student employability, were seen as very important – important by students in relation to potential employers.

Focus groups highlighted the feeling that WBL had enhanced students' experience, skills and knowledge in relation to potential employability.

When asked in the focus groups what was the difference between skills, knowledge and experience there were a number of different responses related to working within a real world environment. One student commented:

> Experience is the best one – you could know everything, have done every course under the sun but if you go into an inner-city high school without experience you could struggle. Experience is more hands on. You're doing rather than being taught, you find out the best way of doing things from experience.

Summary of student data for academic year 2006–07 (pre work-based learning placement)

❑ 89% of respondents stated that they knew what employability is, while 94% consider that employability is important in relation to their learning and development on the course.

❑ 86% of students considered that the skills that they learnt on the course were very important or important to potential employers.

❑ 75% thought knowledge gained on the course was very important or important, while 83% felt that the experiences they would encounter would be very important or important to potential employers.

❑ 69% felt the degree is enabling them to develop their skills, 70% developing their knowledge and 69% believe the degree is enabling them to develop relevant experience.

When comparing the data from 05–06 to 06–07

❑ There is a suggestion that students understand employability but we need to continue to raise the level of awareness and be more explicit with our students within the curriculum, pre and post work-based learning and through career development seminars.

❑ Students recognise the importance of experience, skills and knowledge to potential employers.

❑ Students express an understanding of the differences between experience, skills and knowledge.

❑ It would seem that there is no significant difference between these points pre- and post- placement.

Summary of employer data

According to the Higher Education Academy (2006) employers want recruits who are going to be effective in a changing world. They want people who can deal with change – indeed who thrive on it. They want intelligent, flexible adaptable employees who are quick to learn. In order for a programme to remain current and relevant for the wider world of work, it is imperative that there is an understanding of the needs of the potential employers. This study set out to discover what employers of sports development graduates wanted from potential recruits.

The findings from the questionnaire carried out in 2005–06 generally concurred with existing findings available in relation to employability and the needs of generic employers. 20% of respondents stated they were not content with the knowledge, skills and capabilities of graduates.

Ninety-six percent of respondents considered WBL as important or very important, with almost 70% considering the ability to 'hit the ground running' as important/very important. Occupational skills were also considered important/very important (86%).

The skills that employers felt were the most relevant or very relevant were organisational skills (98.2%), development focus (96.4%), self-confidence (93.9%) and action planning (92.8%).

The Work-Based Learning (WBL) Management Group

Members of the WBL Management Group were asked the following questions:

1   Do you feel that the WBL Management Group is a good idea? Why?
2   What do you believe your role in the group is?
3   How do you see the group developing?
4   Any other comments?

Respondents stated that the WBL Group allows the industry and the university to set up good links and communication. This allows the course to develop and meet the needs of a rapidly evolving employment context. Comments were also made in relation to the currency of the programme and that the group allowed members to keep up with changes as opposed to reacting to them in hindsight. Further responses focused on the diversity of the group and the fact that the members coming from a wide range of organisations, both in their delivery and location, allowed members to share good practice, discuss problems and create positive networks.

When questioned about their role in the group, comments ranged from helping to develop the course, delivery of sport, health and physical exercise in the geographical area, helping deliver good work placement opportunities, and contributing towards research.

When asked how the group may develop, respondents indicated that a smaller steering group and a larger partnership network group may be a good direction to take. CPD for employers was an area that members of the group were keen to explore, as was taking part in research projects.

Using Blackboard discussion boards to support student learning

We have developed the use of Blackboard discussion boards to support our current Level 3 students while they were out on placement, and we sought to use the data from the pre/post evaluation with this same cohort completed in 05–06.

In one session we shared with the cohort the results from the session they had been involved in the previous year to collect pre- and post-WBL data and asked them to consider how their perceptions, skills and knowledge had changed since placement at Level 2 and whether the placement at Level 2 had influenced any decisions surrounding their uptake of the WBL module at Level 3

Comments included:

> With regards to the results of the poll, my views are similar ...in that I thought I knew what was required of the successful candidate as long as they were clued up on what the position entailed. However, I'm beginning to change my perception based upon the experiences gained throughout the WBL module. For example, the ability to be self-driven, assertive, and confident that any task, problem or dream is achievable is the key, and not merely the possession of the relevant knowledge. This is because of the fact that being open to new experiences and willingness to learn is a priceless quality.

> Last year my work-based learning did not go to plan and I found myself dependant on other people, therefore I have created my own project with a little guidance. This encouraged me to meet my own goals, whereas I can be aware of what is happening and what is going wrong. If the project was going wrong, I would be the only one to blame. The skills I have developed as a result are those such as networking, communication and organisation (of my diary).

> Since Level 2 I think I have developed as a person in many ways, such as my confidence has grown and I'm not worried about asking for help if I don't understand something. My communication skills have also improved.

It can be seen from these responses that Level 2 WBL has had an impact on this cohort's perceptions, and it would appear that the students' understanding relating to employability has improved as a consequence of WBL. All respondents stated that they thought they understood what employers were looking for when it came to skills, knowledge and experience but considered that their WBL placements had altered their perceptions because of the 'real life' application required in the work place. All students stated that Level 2 WBL had a positive impact on them and had affected their decision to choose WBL at Level 3.

In a second session the following week we shared the employer data with the cohort and asked the students to reflect on these results with reference to the following:

❑ Do you think these results are a fair reflection of graduate employability?

❑ If you were attending an interview what evidence could you bring from your placement and in general to show that you have the skills they are looking for?

Responses included:

although graduates may have a lot of knowledge and a wide understanding for the area if they do not have work experience then they may struggle as this would make them less confident in the interviews.

I feel that work experience is a very valuable part of learning and looks extremely good on your CV as it shows that you have done the job before and you know what it entails; therefore having the upper hand on someone who has better grades but has no experience in the working environment.

In order to show an organisation that I have the skills for the job, and I am exactly what they are looking for, I would bring my WBL project from this year and last in order for them to see what I achieved while on placement. In these files there are some lesson plans, WBL objectives, strengths and weaknesses and it gives an overall evaluation of how my placements went.

Another respondent merits quoting at length, stating:

I think the stats do provide a true image of graduate employability since the emphasis within many institutions is based upon academic rather than practical perspectives and understandings of the working environment ... Self-development in this respect is stifled since many students believe that throughout their university career they must always relate their opinion to previous studies, research and academic theory. This leaves little to no room for the student to become innovative, and to therefore take the initiative since it has been drilled into them to always relate to others' work.

As a result, I believe that students tend to take fewer risks and so have an under developed understanding of the practicalities of the working environment. This may lead to a decrease in self-confidence. As I suggested in week 11's discussion I have only recently come to learn the importance of being assertive and to drive forward for things you really want. If this message is portrayed at an interview then I believe that the individual who does so is far more likely to be successful than the individual with the stronger academic background. Qualifications are not the 'be all and end all'. Experience, confidence, drive, ambition and a willingness to learn appear much more valued by the prospective employer.

A comment from another student offers the following insight into their thinking:

I may sound like I don't want to achieve the highest possible grade in my studies but that is not the case and it is key for the graduate to maintain a degree of balance between academic and practical attainment. This is the message I would attempt to convey when being interviewed.

The above responses show an insightful level of thinking and offer a number of interesting points for further exploration.

In summary, the creation of the WBL Management Group was a positive step in enhancing the development of the curriculum and enabling the currency and innovation on which we pride ourselves to continue apace. However it is crucial that we do not 'rest on our laurels' and with new programme developments comes a need for reflection and subsequent action to continue this work.

It can be seen that the perceptions of the students were positively affected over the course of this project. The Level 3 cohort demonstrated further understanding and an aptitude for critical thinking when questioned on employability and the value of their work-based learning in their own development.

The findings from our project in relation to employers concur with industry thinking at the time of writing. The calibre of graduates and their knowledge, skills and understanding are critical in terms of the creation of an 'employable' graduate, a point integral to this project.

Benefits to end-users

The benefits may be summarised by considering the four objectives of the study:

1   To examine employer views/opinions on the graduate employability skills they require.
2   To develop a work-based learning discussion forum involving all stakeholders.
3   To examine the views and opinions of students on the related to work-based learning and employability.
4   To disseminate findings of the case study to inform our own and our partners professional practice.
5   To establish a programme of career development seminars to enhance students' employability.

Discussion
Enablers that helped practice to work

A committed programme team enabled this project to be completed, with staff willing and able to devote dedicated time to this project. A strong WBL/Work-Related Learning (WRL) ethos was already an integral part of the Sport Development with PE programme. It was as a consequence of this that changes were easily made to the structure of the WBL induction package.

As a programme team, previous partnership working had been undertaken with

Perceived benefits

For students...	For staff...
Identification of skills employers required from a graduate	Employers involved in the placement-induction process and gaining an insight into higher education
A positive contribution from WBL to the development of students' transferable skills	WBL Management Group has led to the development of a more relevant curriculum
Interventions helped students adapt to the real world of work	Opportunities to collaborate more closely with employers
Students became aware that placements can offer real opportunities for them to decide on a future career path	Establishing clear goals and providing support for student learning is likely to be associated with increased student satisfaction and the development of generic skills
Students were better prepared for the WBL placement	Recognition that individual student's goals are important in the WBL placement
Students better able to reflect on their goals on placement	Peer feedback given to assist in goal-setting often better received than from a tutor
An ability to apply knowledge and use it to solve practical, real-life problems	Student-led group work can assist student in preparation for and throughout their placement
Working in groups helps when going into the work place	Opportunity to enhance the quality of students' reflection considered fundamental to the quality of learning
Peer feedback given to assist in goal setting	Project created extra networking opportunities for the programme team
Students encouraged to work independently	Online discussion boards as part of WBL at Level 3, developed greater opportunities for reflection from students

many of the key stakeholders: local communities, national governing bodies, local employers, and local authorities. Consequently an excellent working relationship had been developed between us and some of the partners who later became involved in the FDTL project. It was important however that communication to inform partners at every stage about rationale, developments and anticipated outcomes occurred regularly.

The establishment of the WBL Management Group (referred to as 'forum' in the initial aims of this project) undoubtedly ensured the project developed at a pace. The members of the Group expressed an interest in becoming involved in other

Issues/Challenges

For students...	For staff...
A perception of too much theory not enough practice	Determining what is an achievable scope in goal-setting and how best learning is to be articulated, assessed, and evaluated
Enhancing employability awareness for the students prior to WBL placement	Training and guidance on 'what learning objectives are?'
Many students do not have clear knowledge or understanding of their career path	Problems of engaging whole-group responsibility for the tasks
Students often change their mind about careers, placements and learning goals	Commitment of other initiatives impacted on time spent on FTDL project
	Trialling new practice is often difficult, as occasionally things are not as successful as hoped
	❑ Measuring success is difficult. The benefit of many of these interventions may not be seen for years
	❑ Creating a balance between theory and practice
	❑ Not enough time to complete all the objectives set
	❑ Revisit the induction activities, although much improved, could still be better

areas of the project such as WBL induction which certainly added value to the worth of the group.

Achieving CETL status during the course of the project meant the project team were able to draw on the expertise of a new member of support staff, who was part of the new CETL team.

The Community Support Officer joined the WBL Management Group and afforded support and assistance relating to the changes in induction at Level 3 and the development of Level 3 discussion boards.

Importantly, one of the key 'enablers' that helped in the achievement of project outcomes were the Sports Development PE students themselves. The students at all times welcomed changes that would provide a better learning experience. They participated in focus groups, interactive questionnaires and discussion boards. Students were not inhibited about sharing their concerns or expectations, and in particular welcomed the opportunity to meet and discuss future development and enhancement.

Points of advice
Consider the amount of staff time dedicated to the project
Three members of staff and one support staff member were involved in the intervention and its outcomes. This would not have been sustainable over a longer period. Consequently small interventions would have to be delivered if commitment could not be assured from this number of staff. As the project and its aims were built into a particular WBL aspect of the curriculum, as a team we could provide a supporting rationale for this time commitment.

Ensure the use of research to inform practice
It goes without saying that research evidence can provide valid and useful evidence about what helps to make programmes work. We were able to identify issues that could be prioritised for action, and then we could identify the factors needed for successful implementation.

Be cautious, to an extent
An excellent relationship has developed between us and our external partners, but unfortunately this is the one area that is difficult to control. Often external partners have different agendas, different timescales and differing expectations, resulting occasionally in frustration and breakdowns in communication. As a programme team we learnt early on that flexibility must be built into any project. We changed or amended some of our overall project outcomes due to fluctuating situations and resources. Another point in fact involves the need for acceptance that interventions that are put into place may not always be suitable. It is important to develop activities, to evaluate them and then revisit their appropriateness.

Change management should not be underestimated
Before undertaking an intervention, discussions must take place within the programme/team as to how much change you are prepared to accept. There are arguments for either radical change or incremental change. Earlier on it was our philosophy that we needed to change things quickly and radically. This of course had significant implications for us and along with that came an acceptance that not everything will be successful. Importantly we recognised we could learn from setbacks.

Possible improvements/enhancers

One of the initial project aims was the delivery of career development seminars for students. This aim was not achieved and must therefore be revisited. It is the intention of the project team to identify a comprehensive programme of these seminars as an integral part of the next academic year.

Further research needs to be undertaken as to the effectiveness of some of the interventions, such as the online discussion boards for Level 3 WBL. As a part of the CETL, researchers will assist in the development of this area.

A more formal curriculum link with our careers colleagues in the university will be pursued, whereby these colleagues can assist with aspects of the induction for WBL, especially at Level 2. Enhancements to PDP at Level 2 will also compliment this work.

There is a need for a continued expansion of both the composition and role of the WBL Management Group. It is envisaged that this forum should become an integral part of our programme's development. There is a willingness and desire by employers to become more involved with the curriculum and the relationships built are strong. The research undertaken as a part of this project suggests that involving employers in decision-making processes relating to work placements met with an excellent response as they wanted to contribute to the debate on this subject. The WBL Management Group can generate exciting ideas about education and its relevance to the workplace. Close links with employers through this forum can ensure currency of the curriculum and further innovative approaches can be promoted by the programme team.

The case study has also identified some areas of development that will be followed in terms of the induction of students prior to placement. It is envisaged that the induction period pre-placement should be lengthened to a six-week programme (three weeks currently). The induction content can be expanded and particular attention can be paid to the development and production of student's personal learning objectives, placement goals, and the placement learning agreement.

External/internal commentary

A comment from member of the WBL Management Group:

> I have been involved in partnership work with LJMU Department for Sport, Dance & Outdoor Education WBL Group for a number of years. I feel that the group has worked closely to influence and steer the direction of the course to ensure that the content of the degree is relevant to the current work climate. I have made some useful contacts through the group and feel it is a good place to share ideas and experiences.

The department have provided me with some excellent students for work placement and as part of research projects. I feel that this is partly due to the relationships that has been created between employers and the university allowing them to
match suitable students to placements and projects. This allows everyone to gain
from the process.

A comment from a colleague who is part of the same programme team, but not
involved in the research:

The project has impacted upon students and staff in a number of ways. Firstly, it
has given the programme the opportunity to audit existing work-related learning
practices in conjunction with external partners and students. This has resulted
in curriculum development in response to the feedback received. Secondly, the
project has given the programme team a focus for developing work-related learning and provided opportunities for enhancement of personal tutoring to students
while out on placement. Thirdly the project has enabled the programme team to
link with other HEI providers to share existing practices.

A comment from Level 3 student undertaking WBL option module:

Having carried out WBL in Level 2, I came to realise the importance of my key
skills and experience to my future employability. Having then chosen to do the
optional module at Level 3 I felt I could better understand the need to audit my
skills. I have found the Blackboard discussion board really useful and my placement provider [a member of the WBL Management Group] has really helped me
with great guidance and support. The induction for Level 3 WBL was better this
year as well.

Further comments

Throughout this project it was always a key objective to disseminate the research
findings, both externally as part of the FDTL project but additionally within our
own institution. In particular we see these data gathered as being of relevance to
colleagues within our faculty. To that end we have already presented the findings
and recommendations to colleagues as part of our LJMU Teaching and Learning
Conference this academic year (2006–07), along with numerous other conferences
and forums. Brief presentations have also been delivered to colleagues in LJMU
who see employability as a key outcome of our teaching. This is of course a developmental process. Although the project has come to an end, it is inevitable (and
desirable) that we will continue with the process of change and evaluation.

Discussion is already taking place about how further research can impact on our
delivery of the employability agenda. Links with our colleagues in Careers have been
established and planning days have taken place to take all of this further. Perhaps in

considering the work of Smith and Betts (2000) this last sentence can best sum up our project evaluation:

> We should move away from learning about work, which is informational; learning at work, which is vocational; and move towards learning through work, which is experiential.

References

Blackwell, A., Bowes, L., Harvey, L., Hesketh, A. and Knight P. T. (2001) Transforming Work Experience in Higher Education. *British Educational Research Journal* **26** (3) pp. 269–86

Cowan, J. (1998) *On Becoming an Innovative University Teacher*. Buckingham: Open University Press

Harvey, L., Moon, S. and Geall, V. with Bower, R. (1997) *Graduates' work: organisational change and students' attributes*. Birmingham: Centre for Research into Quality, University of Central England, Birmingham and the Association of Graduate Recruiters

Harvey, L., Geall, V. and Moon, S. (1998) *Work experience: expanding opportunities for undergraduates*. Birmingham: Centre for Research into Quality, University of Central England in Birmingham

Higher Education Academy (2006) *Employability Tools – What Do Employers Want From Graduates?*, viewed: 15 January 2006 http://www.heacademy.ac.uk/resources/

Little, B., Harvey, L., Moon, S., Marlow-Hayne, N., and Pierce, D. (2002) *Nature and extent of undergraduates' work experience*. Bristol: Higher Education Funding Council for England

Little, B. and ESECT colleagues (2006) Employability and work based learning. *Learning and Employability Series One*. Higher Education Academy

LJMU (2006) *LJMU Plus Implementation Guide: Work Related Learning and Graduate Skills*, viewed: 8 June 2007. http://ljmu.ac.uk/ljmuplus/85381.htm

Moon, J. (2004) Employability and Experiential Learning. *Link* **11** Higher Education Academy for Hospitality, Leisure, Sport and Tourism, pp. 2–3

SkillsActive (2006) *Sport and Recreation*, viewed: 5 February 2006. http://www.skillsactive.com/sportrec

Smith, R. and Betts, M. (2000) Learning as Partners: Realising the Potential of Work-based Learning. *Journal of Vocational Education & Training: The Vocational Aspect of Education*, **52** (4) pp. 589–604

Yorke, M. (2006) *Employability in higher education: what it is – what it is not*. Learning and Employability Series One. York: HEA – Enhancing Student Employability Co-ordination Team

Yorke, M. and Knight, P. T. (2006) *Embedding employability into the curriculum*. Learning and Employability Series One. York: HEA – Enhancing Student Employability Co-ordination Team

2

Entrepreneurship in sport

Karen Bill *University of Worcester*

**This case study explores the links between developing students'
entrepreneurial capabilities and their employability**

This case study provides an overview of the development and delivery of an undergraduate module *Entrepreneurship in Sport* and evaluates its impact on students' employability. This Level 3 module has been piloted with two cohorts of students (2005–06 and 2006–07) studying for the BSc Sports Studies at the University of Worcester. A key aim of the module is to develop students' entrepreneurial capabilities and, thus enhance their problem-solving skills, readiness for change, creativity and self-confidence – all key employability attributes (Henry et al, 2003; Yorke and Knight, 2006). The module runs over a 15-week semester and includes a combination of lectures, small group seminars and on-line tutorials. Taught sessions draw on innovative and creative means of engaging students in the learning process. Assessment on the module consists of an individual written case study, a group presentation ('pitch') of a business idea made to a panel of entrepreneurial 'experts', and a personal statement outlining competencies and capacity for entrepreneurship.

Data on impact has been gathered using a variety of self-assessment tools and questionnaires. Findings indicate that students studying on the module showed an overall improvement in motivation for study, an increase in personal self-esteem and the development of a range of 'enterprise' skills. Student feedback was very positive and several stated that the module had opened up career possibilities that they had previously not been aware of. Tutors felt that students were able to better articulate their employability skills and also reported that the module has been significantly developmental for them as educators. Adapting generic teaching and learning materials on entrepreneurship for the sport subject area has been challenging but has proved important for student engagement with the module.

Objectives

1   To design and validate a level 3 undergraduate module *Entrepreneurship in Sport* for delivery in academic year 2005–06.
2   To develop and incorporate a blend of traditional and online teaching and learning resources in the delivery of the module.
3   To evaluate the impact of the module on students' development of entrepreneurial skills and enhancement of their employability.

Context/rationale

The development of the module featured in this case study is very timely in light of recent government drives to encourage more entrepreneurship teaching in schools/universities, and the desire to equip graduates with the necessary skills to operate effectively in a knowledge economy. In response to the influential Dearing Report in 1997, a key statement to come out of the DfEE document *Higher Education for the 21st Century* (1998) was Recommendation 40 which stated:

> We recommend to higher education institutions that they consider the scope for encouraging entrepreneurship through innovative approaches to programme design and through specialist postgraduate programmes.

Such recommendations have not been made in isolation. The Chancellor of the Exchequer stated in his 2006 Budget Address (and in the Mansion House Speech of 2002) that:

> too few skilled employees, too few men and women are starting and growing businesses – the greatest constraint on the growth of Britain's productivity and prosperity today is now our failure to realise the educational and entrepreneurial potential of our own people.

It would appear that demand for entrepreneurial behaviours in graduates is increasing. Not only is this the case for those who would like to set up their own business – a 2004 Nat West survey indicated that over 57% of University students would consider setting up their own business after finishing their education. But it is also the case that changing career patterns require graduates who are able to move within the employment market in 'entrepreneurial' ways in order to cope with uncertainty and constant change. Graduates in today's world are required to demonstrate innovative approaches to Problem-solving, high readiness for change, self-confidence, and creativity – all attributes related to entrepreneurship. According to Henry et al (2003), 'the need for entrepreneurship education has never been greater, and the opportunities have never been so abundant'. The establishment of the National Council for Graduate Entrepreneurship in 2004, and the publication of several influential reports including; the Lambert *Review of Business–University Collaboration* (2003), the Roberts Report (2003), and the more recent Lord Sainsbury Review (2007), have started to outline an agenda for facilitating a more entrepreneurial culture in universities. The focus is on the development of graduates who can operate effectively in the economy of the future.

Within the context of sport, the sports industry is worth some £9.8 billion a year to the economy and it needs graduates with the critical thinking, entrepreneurial attitude and business skills for managing a successful career. In 2004 the UK sport and recreation industry employed a workforce of 363,100 people (Experian, 2005) working in 25,000 organisations, of which 82% of those employed worked in small or micro businesses. Significant sectoral growth is forecast, with a projected increase in the workforce of 442,500 by 2012. An increased trend towards self-employment amongst students coupled with high levels of sector employment occurring within small firms, mean that the development of employability and entrepreneurial attributes has never been more relevant.

There is strong evidence that sports departments within institutions should begin to acknowledge the thrust for developing entrepreneurial skills in graduates. In 2005 the School of Sport and Exercise Science at the University of Worcester (UoW) responded to this agenda by appointing a member of staff to a dedicated 'Enterprise' post. The purpose of the appointment was to develop an enterprise culture within the School and to encourage students and staff to engage in curriculum development activities that would deliver this aim. The FDTL5 project on Enhancing Graduate Employability which also began in 2005, therefore acted as a catalyst for developing an undergraduate module entitled *Entrepreneurship in Sport*.

At an institutional level, one of the UoW's five strategic objectives is to produce

Figure 1 Framework for entrepreneurial activities

High-level plan

	Year 1 Awareness	Year 2 Interest		Year 3 Decision	Graduation Action
ECP	Enterprise Fest (delegate) Taster workshop in idea development	Enterprise Fest (delegate) 15-credit vocational enterprise module	Enterprise Summer School	Enterprise Fest (exhibitor) BizCom Graduate Enterprise	Enterprise Fest (speaker) EFS InvoRed
WIN	Junior member of development team	The Ideas Generator		Individuals and teams building business proposals	Mentoring CPD Student placement

highly employable, innovative, and professional alumni (UoW Strategic Plan, 2004–08). Enterprise education constitutes a key aspect of this and the university has developed a series of entrepreneurship activities designed to engage students throughout their degree programmes, and post-graduation (see Figure 1). The intervention outlined in this case study, the *Entrepreneurship in Sport* module, works within this framework and builds on these institutional activities.

Description
The module

The Level 3 *Entrepreneurship in Sport* module has been piloted with two cohorts of students (2005–06 and 2006–07) studying for a BSc Hons Sports Studies at the University of Worcester. A key aim of the module is to develop students' entrepreneurial capabilities. The module runs over a 15-week semester and includes a combination of lectures, small group seminars and on-line tutorials covering the topics outlined in Table 1.

Table 1 *Entrepreneurship in Sport* module overview

Lecture	Seminar (WebCT)
What is an entrepreneur/entrepreneurship?	Am I an entrepreneurial type (online quiz)
The importance of entrepreneurship to HLST	Profiles of sports entrepreneurs
Motivations for starting a business – Push and Pull	Do I have the right personal skills for success Shell Livewire (personal profile)?
Generating a business idea	Stretch your mind (start talking ideas)
Team roles and responsibilities	Drama – The Aquarium
The route to market	SimsVenture software
Customers / marketing strategy	Enterprise Week – Make your mark challenge
Financial needs of the business	Cash flow – can I make a profit?
Presentation skills – What is an elevator pitch?	Dragons Den review
Bizcom/SPEED preparation	

Lectures are delivered by a mixture of academic staff and sports entrepreneurs, and the online aspects of the module (WebCT based) have been customised for sports students. Taught sessions draw on innovative and creative means of engaging students in the learning process. For example, drama is used in one of the seminars (*The Aquarium*) to enable students to role-play in a 'safe' environment and to explore hidden aspects of the self that may be relevant to their inner motivations and capacity for entrepreneurship.

The assignment

Assessment on the module consists of an individual written case study in which students are required to evaluate the business performance of a sports entrepreneur of their choosing using appropriate theory to support their analysis. The second part of the assessment is a group presentation of a business idea made to a panel of 'experts' made up of academic staff, sports entrepreneurs and staff from the University's business partnerships office. Students are required to 'pitch' their business idea to the expert panel in much the same way as in the popular TV programme *Dragon's Den* and they support this with a written business plan/report. An added dimension to the module is the encouragement for students to submit their business plan to competitions such as Bizcom and SPEED which are national business competitions aimed at students (students participating in this case study were successful in winning these competitions with their ideas being awarded prizes of £2,000 and £6,000 in 2005–06). Finally students are asked to provide a personal statement, outlining their skills and competencies for entrepreneurship.

An entrepreneurial, directed approach to teaching and learning

The teaching of entrepreneurship in the university context is based on theoretical and practical knowledge of this subject area. A key dimension of the learning approach is the very active role the student plays in the process. Kyro (2003) suggests that the bridges between entrepreneurship and education should be stronger in order to make the pedagogy more robust (i.e. the process is as relevant as the subject). Kirby (2002) goes so far as to suggest that traditional approaches to learning may actually inhibit the development of entrepreneurial attributes as they ignore the essence of the entrepreneurial process.

In designing this module it became apparent that when teaching about entrepreneurialism, it is fundamental for the lecturer to infuse entrepreneurial characteristics such as **opportunity recognition** and **creativity** into the classroom. A key premise is that anyone is capable of entrepreneurial activity once she/he has given her/himself permission to be brave, creative and innovative. *The Aquarium*, outlined above and taken from Heinonen and Poikkijoki (2006), enables students to critically examine and evaluate entrepreneurial skills, attributes and behaviours in a team environment. This entrepreneurial directed role-playing technique gives students the opportunity to assume a new role and to probe hidden aspects of the self while learning about the concept of entrepreneurial behaviour (Sogunro, 2004).

IT support for the module

The *Entrepreneurship in Sport* module has been heavily supported by a comprehensive

WebCT site which contains a wide range of interactive online resources. The format includes discussion groups, online tests, online surveys, lecture notes and exercises. The website also provides a useful vehicle to enable students to undertake practical exercises which build on the in-class learning and further enhance the impact of the module learning.

Evaluation

Data on impact of the module on participants was gathered using a variety of tools. These included an Intrinsic Motivation Inventory (IMI) questionnaire, Rosenberg's 10-item Self-Esteem Scale questionnaire (Rosenberg, 1989) and a module feedback questionnaire completed by students. The data indicates that students studying on the module showed an overall improvement in their motivation for study, an increase in personal self-esteem and a development in 'enterprise' skills. Student feedback on the module was very positive and they reported feeling more informed about the skills required for employability/entrepreneurship. Several students also stated that the module had opened up career opportunities that they had previously not been aware of, or had not thought about. The tutors involved in the intervention felt that students were able to better articulate their employability skills, and also reported that the module has been hugely developmental for them as educators.

Mid- and end-module evaluation

Student feedback on the lecture content and the WebCT site/links was very positive. Students indicated the module had aided their understanding of the world of the entrepreneur. One student noted:

> Before this module started my knowledge was very limited and to be honest I had no interest in it. This however has changed throughout and I now feel that I have learnt a great deal about how to go about starting a business. This new found knowledge and interest came from things such as guest speakers talking about their own enterprises.

Other student comments included:

> I have learnt more employability skills that I didn't feel I was good at before.
> Studying an extremely interesting subject, with a variety of methods, extremely enjoyable.
> This module is by far the best module I have ever done while at Uni. The module is an excellent idea. I thoroughly enjoyed it all.

Students responded positively to the assessment format commenting that assignment two provided them with the opportunity to 'get a chance to pitch our own ideas instead of writing them all down in an assignment; creating a name, designing, etc. was really ... good fun'.

Student feedback from the first cohort highlighted a desire for an increased amount of sport application in the teaching delivery/materials used on the module. In response to this feedback the tutor invited a sports entrepreneur into the University to speak to the students, and she also secured funding to develop a sports entrepreneur educational DVD. Students in the second cohort reacted very positively to the visiting sports entrepreneur, noting:

> the entrepreneurs coming in to speak to us. This was very interesting to listen to someone who has made their own business.
>
> it was a totally different aspect of sport to look at.
>
> it has given me an insight into how business works, and increased my business knowledge and knowhow vastly and greatly!

It is evident that students benefited from contextualising entrepreneurship within sport which has significant potential to impact positively on their learning.

Self-esteem scale

Rosenberg's ten-item Self-Esteem Scale questionnaire (SES) was distributed pre- and post-module to explore potential change in students' self-esteem in relation to the module. Rosenberg's Self-Esteem Scale (Rosenberg, 1989) is reportedly the most widely used self-esteem measure in social science research (see Appendix 1 for results). The findings for both case study cohorts demonstrate that student perceptions of their self-esteem increased from the beginning to the end of the module. Anecdotally the module leader observed a noticeable increase in self-confidence and achievement across a number of students. Given that self-confidence is viewed as a very important employability attribute, it would be beneficial for further research to explore this and to seek student testimonies which may provide a richer account and greater insight into the impact of the module.

Intrinsic Motivation Inventory

A pre- and post-evaluation questionnaire was adapted for the module based on the Intrinsic Motivation Inventory scale (IMI) to investigate student motivation. The IMI is an multidimensional measurement device designed to explore the intrinsic motivation of individuals (McAuley, Duncan and Tammen, 1989). Findings indicated that both the students' interest/enjoyment and perceived competency subscales of IMI increased from beginning to end of the module (see Appendix 1).

Statistical confirmation of an increase in interest/enjoyment and perceived competency within a module suggests that the learning and teaching process was effective. Indeed it would be slightly alarming to find that the student experience was not so positive. Equally the pressure/tension subscale of IMI increased from pre to post which aligns possibly with the typical experience that module assessment traditionally occurs at the end of the process, and students were waiting for their module grades at the time of the post-measure. The second part of the assessment, which was the elevator pitch, was evidenced as being particularly challenging for the students in relation to generating a business idea and working as part of a team.

Group performance profile

Students also completed a performance profile to explore changes in their perceived entrepreneurial skills (Butler, 1993) and the extent to which they had developed/improved these skills.

The group performance profile results with the first student cohort (see Appendix 2) illustrated that the students initially had a narrow perception of what entrepreneurial skills were, but by the post-test they had expanded and redefined many of the initial constructs. In fact they almost created a further subset of employability skills akin to entrepreneurship, such as innovation and a business mind. It was particularly noticeable that leadership and communication skills had increased from pre to post-test. The sports psychology lecturer involved in the delivery of the module noted:

> It was quite exciting to use performance profiling to investigate entrepreneurial behaviours. The students, as expected, had a wider understanding of what sort of descriptors to use at the end of the module. However, their prioritisation of these characteristics and their scoring was interesting; while the measures were not specific to entrepreneurs, it is encouraging to see that these results could be used to interpret behaviour in this area. (Julia West, 2007)

In terms of the second cohort, their pre-test profile indicated a much wider range of entrepreneurial skills which remained similar through to post-test. This could be due, in part, to the increased media exposure over the last year to enterprise type challenges such as *The Apprentice* and *Dragon's Den*.

Discussion

This case study has been immensely rewarding for all those involved, students and teachers alike. It has led to the creation of a range of teaching materials and resources that can be used by other sports educators in the teaching of entrepreneurship. Furthermore it has demonstrated that generic material in this area can be adapted for use in any subject and with any group of students.

Benefits to end users

Perceived benefits	
For students...	**For staff...**
Students felt that the intervention gave them new career options and made them think about their future. In terms of skills, one student noted *'I have learnt more quality skills that I didn't feel I was good at before.'* The students expressed the view that the intervention had increased their self-confidence as well as providing an opportunity to make new friends A further potential benefit is associated with the opportunity to explore business ideas in a 'safe environment' and to learn about the financial aspects of running a business	Experimenting with more enterprising ways of delivery and a move away from the more didactic approaches of teaching Inbuilt staff development – teaching on a module like this offers the tutor opportunities to engage with entrepreneurship-related activities alongside the students Teaching on a module where it is possible to notice a visible positive change in students' development and confidence is an extremely rewarding experience The opportunity to work alongside students as they develop business ideas is an exciting experience providing the tutor with new learning and insight into their students' creativity
Issues/Challenges	
For students...	**For staff...**
Potential challenges facing the students relate to generating a business idea, working as part of a team, undertaking honest self-evaluation and overcoming anxieties about a lack of business acumen. Many of these issues were addressed throughout the module and the students surmounted them with the support of tools and techniques embedded in the course	The lack of publications/resources on sports entrepreneurship posed challenges to contextualising the teaching materials The personal challenge in terms of new delivery methods that are more entrepreneurial and dynamic Dealing with student anxiety in terms of their business knowledge and being able to generate business ideas Trying to find robust tools/questionnaires, rather than relying on subjective opinion and observation, that can provide reliable data to demonstrate the impact that this type of module has on students' self-confidence

Enablers that helped practice to work

❑ FDTL5 funding was used to leverage match funding from TE3 (Technology Enhanced Enterprise Education fund) to develop this module on WebCT.

❑ Collaborative synergies with fellow FDTL5 partners, in particular colleagues at Liverpool John Moores University and the University of Gloucestershire, allowed us to bounce around ideas and exchange information on teaching approaches/resources.

❑ Collaboration with institutional colleagues. Julia West, sports psychology lecturer, provided significant support exploring self efficacy and motivational changes in the students.

❑ Embedding the module within institutional practices, and enabling students to enter national competitions such as Bizcom and SPEED. A student team from the first cohort won first prize in the Enterprise Award at Bizcom, and a group of students from the second cohort won a SPEED placement to develop their business idea further.

❑ Involving entrepreneurs in the assessment process has been of substantial benefit to the students involved. During the second run of the module, one group presenting caught the attention of a sports entrepreneur involved in the course and they are currently negotiating mentoring support as their idea compliments his sport equipment business.

❑ The growth of new forums and conferences around enterprise teaching such as the IEEP provides ideas for innovative teaching resources and has been extremely beneficial in encouraging a more entrepreneurial approach to enterprise education.

Points of advice

When designing the assessment criteria on the module, it has been very beneficial to ensure the assessment activities are portable and capable of being externally recognised, for instance, in business competitions. This has had enormous benefits for both cohorts of students in terms of the module assessment being a gateway to other regional enterprising events and competitions.

The module was validated as a credit-bearing module. This has significant potential in terms of being integrated into other degree programmes. Since validation, this particular module has been included in a BSc Outdoor Recreation Management degree and the BSc Sport Business Management, which makes a clear case for the sustainability of the module and subject material.

As this is a relatively new area, it has been challenging to source sport-related material. Most of the resources and business start-up examples are focused on more generic business. Students can struggle to adapt the material to sport and at times find it challenging to see the direct relevance of it. It is important to be resourceful and source a wide range of materials. The Shell Livewire is just one website which contains an element of sport related material as well as more generic resources.

As this is a new area, it can be difficult to attract students and sometimes sports students are put off by the notion of business. The student numbers, while increasing, have been below the traditional student-staff ratio and it has been problematic to make a case for continued resource support. It is evident that over the two years, this module offered tremendous added value for students that are perhaps not achieving as well on their course overall. Students on the module report increased confidence levels and have excelled in this area. Staff from the University of Worcester business partnership office have been very supportive and commented that:

> Vocational enterprise, that is, enterprise not as a stand-alone skill set but in the context of the learner's vocational interest, is extremely important. Karen Bill's *Enterprise and Innovation in Sport* is our shining example of this. Karen and I are working to extend this model to other Academic Departments.
>
> (Andy Corcoran, 2007)

Possible improvements/enhancers
Possible improvements/enhancers include:
- ❏ Greater use of sports entrepreneurs – currently investigating the possibility of a sports entrepreneur-in-residence appointment.
- ❏ More sports entrepreneurship resources – the development of a sports-entrepreneur DVD is currently in progress.
- ❏ Exploring robust questionnaires to assist the students with their personal profile in terms of entrepreneurial readiness.
- ❏ Identifying robust tools which can test the assumptions that entrepreneurship modules have a positive impact upon the students' employability skills and in particular, self-confidence.

The development of an enhanced understanding of employability
The case study has , I believe, enabled the students' to develop their entrepreneurial capabilities and grow in self-confidence. Many students, informally, have reported that they feel they now possess a 'can-do' attitude. The module has also provided students with opportunities to self-reflect and articulate their employability skills via some of the profiling and tests that have been built into the module. This is often a difficult area for students to verbalise honestly and openly. Furthermore, for many, it had opened up career possibilities, providing them with the 'know-how'

and 'know-who' that they had previously not been aware of. This even led to some going on to start up their own businesses (e.g. Active Opps). Very often we discuss with students where they could get employment rather than how they could shape their own employment by becoming self-employed.

The module has been significantly developmental for me as an educator. It has enabled me to challenge my own lecturing skills in terms of how I am able to become more enterprising in my own delivery if I am expecting students to become more enterprising. It has challenged me to be more explicit about how I attempt to cultivate appropriate employability skills within the module. It is not just about business start-up, but about encouraging a more entrepreneurial mindset within the students.

References

Brown, G. (2002) Mansion House Speech. HM Treasury

Butler, R., Smith, M. & Irwin, I. (1993) The performance profile in practice. *Journal of Applied Sport Psychology* 5, pp. 48–63

Dearing Report (1997) *The Report of the National Committee of Inquiry into Higher Education.* London: DfEE

DfEE (1998) *Higher Education for the 21st Century.* The Government's Response to 'Higher Education in the Learning Society' – The Report of the National Committee of Inquiry into Higher Education, chaired by Sir Ron (now Lord) Dearing

Experian (2005) *Labour Force Survey. Skills Needs Assessment, England 2005*

Heinonen, J. and Poikkijoki, S. (2006) An entrepreneurial-directed approach to entrepreneurship education: mission impossible? *Journal of Management Development* 25 (1)

Henry, C., Hill, F. and Leitch, C. (2003) *Entrepreneurship Education and Training.* Aldershot: Ashgate

Kirby, D. (2002) 'Entrepreneurship education: can business schools meet the challenge?' Paper presented at the RENT XVI Conference, Barcelona, 21–22 November

Kyro, P. (2003), 'Entrepreneurship pedagogy – the current state and some future expectations'. Paper presented at the 3rd European Summer University, Paris, 26 June–3 July

Lord Sainsbury Review (2007) *The Race to the Top. A Review of Government's Science and Innovation Policies.* HM Treasury

McAuley, K., Duncan, T. E. and Tammen, V. V. (1989) Psychometric properties of the Intrinsic Motivation Inventory in a competitive sport setting: A confirmatory factor analysis. *Research Quarterly for Exercise and Sport* 60, pp. 48–58

National Commission on Entrepreunership (2003) *Creating good jobs in your community.* Washington D.C. Available from http://www.ncoe.org/research/4929_NCOE_GUIDE.pdf

Rosenberg, M. (1989) *Rosenberg's 10-item Self Esteem Scale.* The Morris Rosenberg Foundation: Maryland, USA

Sogunro, O.A. (2004) Efficacy of role-playing pedagogy in training leaders: some reflections. *Journal of Management Development* 23 (4) pp. 355–71

Strategic Leisure (2004) *North West Development Agency Sport Business Cluster – Strategy and Action Plan*

Universities UK (2006) *Higher level learning: Universities and employers working together.* November 2006

Yorke, M. and Knight, P. T. (2006) *Embedding employability into the curriculum,* Learning and Employability Series One. York: HEA – Enhancing Student Employability Co-ordination Team

Appendix 1   Self-esteem and intrinsic motivation results

Descriptor	2005 cohort			2006 Cohort		
	N	M	SD	N	M	SD
SES						
Pre	9	28.56	6.13	12	30.17	2.79
Post	6	30.67	4.80	14	30	3.98
IMI Interest/enjoyment						
Pre	9	20.06	6.03	10	17.86	2.7
Post	6	25.30	6.80	14	19.6	5.62
Perceived competency						
Pre	9	20.09	4.81	10	18.05	3.95
Post	6	27.78	2.10	14	22.36	6.54
Perceived choice						
Pre	9	18.75	5.48	10	26.46	4.15
Post	6	16.57	2.14	14	29.79	3.04
Pressure/tension						
Pre	9	27.11	5.03	10	21.83	4.58
Post	6	34.09	4.68	14	27.03	2.14

Key to Table
N   number of participants
M   mean
SD standard deviation

❏ For additional information on Rosenberg's Self-Esteem Scale please
     see http://www.bsos.umd.edu/Socy/Research/Rosenberg.htm
❏ For additional information on the Intrinsic Motivation Inventory please
     see http://www.psych.rochester.edu/SDT/measures/intrins.html

Appendix 2   Performance profile results

Performance profile	2005 Cohort		2006 Cohort	
	Pre	Post	Pre	Post
Risk-taker	7	7	5	4
Confidence	7		6	3
Opportunist	6			
Creative	8	7	5	5
Ambitious	9			
Ability to bounce back	7			
Initiative	9			
Adaptability	8			
Leadership	5	7		3
Problem-solver	8		8	
Motivation	10	9		4
Communication	6	8	6	6
Efficient	7			
Determined		8	10	7
Teamwork		8		4
Business mind		6		
Hard worker		7		
Patience		7		
Innovation		7		
Cooperation		8		
Lateral thinking		6		
Computer skills		6		
Organisation			9	8
Financially aware			7	
Persuasive			4	
Finisher				3
Decision-making			4	3

3

Using PDP to track, audit and evidence employability skills

Deidre A Brennan and Marie H Murphy
University of Ulster at Jordanstown

This case study focuses on the use of a university Personal Development Planning (PDP) system and pre-placement workshops designed to develop students' employability skills.

Objectives

The case study describes an intervention which used the PDP system to encourage Level 2 undergraduate students to:

- Develop an understanding/awareness of employability skills.
- Conduct a personal employability skills audit.
- Learn how to evidence their employability skills.
- Identify opportunities for developing employability skills gaps identified by the skills audit.
- Reflect on their skill development after a year's placement in the sports industry.

Rationale

A degree alone is not enough. Employers are looking for more than just technical skills and knowledge of a degree discipline. They particularly value skills such as communication, teamworking and problem-solving. Job applicants who can demonstrate that they have developed these skills will have a real advantage.

(Digby Jones, 2004)

One of the primary motives for students undertaking higher education is to improve employability. In an increasingly competitive graduate market students need to equip themselves to meet the needs and expectations of prospective employers. Over the past 15 years a considerable literature has identified a range of skills and behaviours that allow graduates to interact and work with people in a variety of situations (Hind and Moss, 2005). These include the traditional skills such as communication, interpersonal and social skills along with newer additions such as numeracy, IT literacy and higher order skills such as problem-solving and critical thinking.

The Work Related Learning Report (2002) by the Department for Education and Skills (DfES) identified the need for HE courses to encourage students to improve their higher-level competencies and skills to enhance their long-term employability and encouraged the integration of work-based and study-based learning. In particular the report highlighted the need to encourage student reflection during the study programme in order that students might identify additional tuition needs and how these might best be satisfied. The DfES report specified the three categories of work experience that a student can use to enhance employability: organised work experience as part of a programme of study, organised work experience external to a programme of study and ad hoc work experience external to a programme of study.

Context

The University of Ulster (UU) is a modern, multi-campus institution that offers a contemporary programme for students, innovation in teaching and research and an established record in providing educational opportunities irrespective of social or religious backgrounds. The University has an enrolment of approximately 24,000 students and is the largest university in Northern Ireland and one of the largest universities on the island of Ireland. Campuses are located in Belfast, Coleraine, Magee, and Jordanstown. A fifth virtual campus, Campus One, provides online learning opportunities.

Sport is a strategic priority of the University and in recognition of this the University launched the University of Ulster Sports Academy in December 2006. The School of Sports Studies came into existence in August 2006 and is the academic division of UU Sports Academy. The school is located in Jordanstown, within the Faculty of Life and Health Sciences. The school currently consists of 15 academic staff supported by technical and administrative staff. The school has over 350 students studying for foundation, undergraduate, and postgraduate research degrees in Sports Studies, Sport & Exercise Sciences and Sports Coaching. The aim is to be the leading institution in Ireland for the study of sport and exercise and to use knowledge and expertise of staff and students for the benefit of the local, national and international community. To achieve this, the school is committed to excellence in three key areas: teaching, research and outreach and academic enterprise.

The majority of students on the BSc (Hons) Sport Studies and BSc (Hons) Sport and Exercise Science degrees undertake a one-year placement for the award of a Diploma in Industrial Studies (DIS). This is however optional, with some students choosing to progress straight to final year. During Year 2 students make decisions on whether or not to undertake a placement and if so, which employer/organisation might best develop their skills. During the year, all students complete a non-credit bearing module to prepare them for placement. At present, although many of our students develop a range of employability skills both within the curriculum and through their extensive extra-curricular voluntary and paid employment, feedback from placement employers indicates that awareness of these 'skills' is very low.

The University of Ulster introduced a PDP package to Year 1 of all undergraduate courses in 2004–05. The system allows students to audit their knowledge and skills in a wide range of areas and build a portfolio of material to evidence their skills.

A programme which increases awareness of students' employability skills and uses the Personal Development System to help them locate, track and evidence these skills would be beneficial for all students. For those about to embark on placement, it would help them choose an appropriate placement and formulate clear objectives, which would allow them to enhance their employability skills while on placement. For students who do not wish to undertake placement, the programme would help them to identify other sources of employability skills in their voluntary and paid employment and their extra curricular activities and identify any gaps which could be addressed before graduation. For both groups of students the PDP programme is designed to help them understand employability skills and to reflect on their acquisition of these skills in a way which is likely to enhance their employment success.

Description
Researchers/staff
Two members of Sports staff designed and implemented the intervention. An additional third member of staff (with no expertise in sport) was the module coordinator of the *Preparation for Placement* module in which the intervention was embedded.
Students
The research group consisted of Year 2 undergraduate Sports Studies and Sport and Exercise Science students (n=100) who were completing a non-credit bearing *Preparation for Placement* module in preparation for a year's industrial placement which, if successfully completed, leads to the award of DIS.
The context
The *Preparation for Placement* module is a compulsory non credit bearing module which offers one hour classes a week over semester 1 and semester 2.
Pre-intervention assessment
Sixty-seven students completed a pre-intervention questionnaire to assess their understanding of employability skills, to rate the importance of these skills and to

indicate the degree to which they believe they have developed these skills.

Intervention

The intervention consisted of four workshop sessions delivered as part of the preparation for placement module:

Workshop 1   *Introduction to PDS and Employability Skills*
Workshop 2   *Conducting your Employability Skills Audit on the PDS*
Workshop 3   *Providing Evidence for the Skills you possess*
Workshop 4   *Finding Opportunities for developing your employability skills*

The University of Ulster Personal Development System (PDS) provides an online generic skills audit instrument for students to assess their competence in employability-skill areas. There are 40 individual skills identified within six employability-skill areas i.e. communication, working with others, application by number, information technology, problem-solving and improving own learning and performance. Students assess their competence in each skill by selecting an appropriate level (1–5). The 5 levels of competence are defined in Table 1.

Table 1   Levels of competence

Level	Description
1	You have no real knowledge or evidence of any meaningful experience in this area
2	You are underdeveloped in this area and have only limited knowledge and understanding of the skill. Your experience will be at a basic level but you can still provide specific supporting evidence
3	You are reasonably competent with some knowledge and understanding of the skill. Your evidence demonstrates that you have some quality experience
4	You are competent with a substantial knowledge and understanding of the skill. Your experience goes well beyond the routine context and you can provide clear and current evidence of your achievements
5	You have a very high level of competence with a comprehensive depth of knowledge and understanding of the skill. Your recent quality evidence demonstrates you have extensive experience in this area

After the first three workshop sessions, students were asked to use the PDS Generic Skills Audit to self-assess the degree to which the employability skill has been acquired and provide evidence of each skill. Once this process was complete, each student received guidance from one of the module tutors to identify remaining employability skills gaps and begin formulating an action plan for acquiring these skills during placement or in final year.

Evaluation

Following the intervention, evaluation was conducted using four methods.

1   Post-intervention assessment

Fifty-five students completed a post intervention questionnaire to explore their understanding of employability skills. When asked to rate the importance of aspects of their course for their career pre-intervention, a large majority of students rated all elements related to work experience as crucial. The questionnaire results indicate that students' perception of the importance of work experience actually increased as a result of participation in this intervention. In particular, the value of undertaking work experience prior to the course was seen as very/quite important by over 87% of students at the end of the intervention as opposed to 75% pre-intervention. In addition, more than 90% of students ranked supervised work experience as important/very important to their future career. These findings are commensurate with evidence contained in the management literature which makes a clear connection between supervised work experience and enhanced student employability (Little and Harvey, 2006). It is interesting to note that both financial management and marketing management were perceived to be relatively less important for future career. Although there was increased awareness of the importance of both post-intervention, still only just over half of the respondents viewed financial management as important/very important. Evaluation of students' skills audit (see Appendix 1) indicates that numeracy is students' weakest skill area and this requires remedial

Table 1   Aspects of course important for future career

Subject area studied	% considering aspect very/quite important to their career		
	Pre-intervention (n=67)	Post-intervention (n=55)	% Change
Operations management	64.2	58.2	−6%
Operation skills	68.7	60.0	−8.7%
Human resource management	58.2	58.3	no change
Financial management	40.3	52.7	+12.4%
Marketing management	29.9	36.4	+6.5%
IT subjects	55.2	61.8	+6.6%
Supervised work experience	82.1	90.9	+8.8%
Prior work experience	74.6	87.3	+12.7%
Work experience portfolio	79.1	67.3t	−11.8%
Dissertation	67.2	69.1	+1.9%

work as application of number is an important skill for career success.

When asked to evaluate the value of their undergraduate degree before and after the intervention, over 90% of respondents reported that their degree would improve career prospects, give them professional credibility and give them advantage over non-graduates. In addition the majority of students rated their degree as useful/very useful in obtaining a job, progressing their career and enhancing their long-term earnings potential. Post-intervention students felt that a degree in sport studies or sport and exercise sciences gave them an advantage over graduates from other disciplines (49% to 73%).

Table 2 Factors influencing career success

Influencing factors	% rating very/quite important for career success		
	Pre-intervention (n=67)	Post-intervention (n=55)	% Change
Social origin	16.4	9.1	−7.3%
Chance	55.2	23.6	−31.6%
Personal ability	97	96.4	−0.6%
Opportunism	77.6	83.6	+6%
Level of education	88.1	90.9	+2.8%
Political influence	43.3	7.3	−36%
Personal achievement	83.6	90.9	+7.3%
Ruthlessness	35.8	40.0	+4.2%
Money	29.4	21.8	−7.6%
Honesty	79.1	76.4	−2.7%
Connections	80.6	67.3	−13.3%
Initiative	97.0	92.7	−4.3%
Organisational ability	97.0	89.1	−7.9%
Professional competence	94.0	92.7	−1.3%
Diligence/industry	65.7	63.6	−2.1%
Self-awareness	65.7	89.6	+23.9%
Self-confidence	89.6	97	+7.4%
Independence	97	97	–
Emotional intelligence	97	86.6	−10.4%
Adaptability	86.6	94	+7.4%
Stress tolerance	94	91	−3%
Initiative	91	97	+6%
Willingness to learn	97	91	−6%
Reflectiveness	91	86.6	−4.4%
Malleable self-theory	86.6	80.6	−6%

When asked to rate the importance of a range of personal qualities for career success, an overwhelming majority of students pre- and post-intervention rated personal ability, initiative, organisational ability, professional competence level and self-confidence as very/quite important with very few indicating that social origin was important in career success. The greatest change from pre- to post-intervention was a decrease in the number of students rating chance as an important factor in career success (from 55% to 23%) and an increase in the rating of the importance of self-awareness (66% to 90%).

When asked to rate the importance of core skills in influencing career success large proportions of the students pre- and post-intervention rate critical analysis, creativity, listening, written communication, explaining and oral presentations as important. Following the intervention there was a large decrease in the extent to which students' rate information retrieval skills as important to career success (73% to 26%). The skills-audit evaluation (see Appendix 1) indicated that students did not feel confident in their ability to create or retrieve information from a database. The scores were particularly low amongst female students and suggest a lack of competence/confidence in the construction and use of databases and this has raised a potential issue for the course team.

When asked to rate the importance of process skills to career success – prioritising, coping with ambiguity and complexity, acting morally, problem-solving, resolving

Table 3 Importance of core skills influencing career success

Core Skills	% rating very/quite important for career success		
	Pre-intervention (n=67)	Post-intervention (n=55)	% Change
Reading effectiveness	74.6	72.7	−1.9%
Numeracy	67.2	67.3	+0.1%
Information retrieval	73.1	25.5	−47.6%
Language skills	25.4	21.8	−3.6%
Self-management	91	90.9	−0.1%
Critical analysis	85.1	87.3	+2.2%
Creativity	85.1	81.8	−3.3%
Listening	88.1	89.1	+1%
Written communication	83.6	81.8	−1.8%
Oral presentations	89.6	90.9	+1.3%
Explaining	91	92.7	+1.7%
Global awareness	56.7	61.8	+5.1%

conflict and teamwork – these were rated important by the great majority of students surveyed. Fewer students rated commercial awareness or political sensitivity as important in this regard. Following the intervention there were only marginal changes in the rated importance of process skills.

Table 4 Importance of process skills influencing career success

Process Skills	% rating very/quite important for career success		
	Pre-intervention (n=67)	Post-intervention (n=55)	% Change
Computer literacy	70.1	76.4	+6.3%
Commercial awareness	50.7	43.6	−7.1%
Political sensitivity	44.8	47.3	+2.5%
Ability to work cross-culturally	74.6	70.9	−3.7%
Ethical sensitivity	73.1	78.2 .	+5.1%
Prioritising	86.6	87.3	−0.7%
Planning	94	94.5	+0.5%
Applying subject understanding	68.7	61.8	−6.9%
Acting morally	89.6	85.5	−4.1%
Coping with ambiguity& complexity	88.1	90.9	+2.8%
Problem-solving	88.1	90.9	+2.8%
Influencing	83.6	76.4	−7.2%
Arguing for or justifying a point	73.1	78.2	+5.1%
Resolving conflict	89.6	87.3	−2.3%
Decision making	92.5	96.4	+3.9%
Negotiating	80.6	76.4	−4.2%
Teamwork	95.5	94.5	−1%

2   Student engagement and PDS skills audit evaluation

Student engagement with the intervention was determined by monitoring attendance at each workshop session, monitoring the number of completed skills-audit returns, the quality of the evidence cited to support individual audits, and the degree to which skills gaps were identified and action plans formulated to address these. A full evaluation of the PDS generic skills audit instruments returned by students is contained in Appendix 1. Students who embarked on a one-year placement following the intervention were asked to complete another generic skills audit and to use the PDS to send this through to the tutors. This was not compulsory and was in addition to the portfolio and project work that students complete as part of the DIS. Unfortunately no students completed this second audit.

3   Intervention evaluation

All students received an evaluation of the intervention by email. Only four students completed and returned this evaluation. These were generally positive reporting increased understanding of employability skills as a result of intervention.

Discussion

The key results of the intervention can be summarised as

1   Students are interested in employability and what will make them more employable as graduates.

2   The time and effort required to complete the generic skills audit evidencing skills, action planning and goal setting is significant. Only 30% of the research group completed the tasks associated with the intervention. We had a nil return on the second personal skills audit.

3   The majority of students will not fully complete the tasks outlined above if there is no academic credit associated with this work.

4   Students may perform better on these tasks if the skills audit was customised to their vocational/professional area i.e. sport.

5   The numerical scoring selected by the students was often too generous for the depth of evidence provided. The scale is such that a respondent could always provide a score of three so as to suggest they are average at the skill and would not consider themselves underdeveloped but are aware there is room for improvement.

6   Students ranked their level of competence in most employability skills as four out of a possible five indicating that as level 2 students in their first semester of year 2 they have already attained a high level of competence in a range of employability skills.

7   The repetition of appropriate evidence across a number of skill areas reinforces the interconnectedness of many work-based and general learning experiences but also perhaps indicates the narrowness of some students experience to date.

8   Application of number was the lowest area of competency identified by the students. Information technology cited the highest competence scoring and displayed the most realistic matching of numerical ratings and evidence. Information technology was the only section where the male students' average mean and mode was greater than the female students. Despite having the highest overall area mean, the lowest recorded mean for any question throughout

the entire skills audit was in the IT section.

9 Students found Problem-solving difficult to evidence.

10 Across the range of students there was inconsistency in understanding what each numerical scoring meant as many students were giving the same evidence but providing different competence scores.

Benefits to end users

Perceived benefits	
For students...	**For staff...**
Opportunity to establish level of skills achieved, collate evidence of abilities and plan for future development	Opportunity to draw on experiences of students in teaching and learning contexts
Ability to use PDP in preparation for job interviews for placement and graduate work opportunities	Opportunity to stay abreast of opportunities in the sports industry
Opportunity to gain advice from staff on potential work-related opportunities that could improve their employment profile	
Issues/Challenges	
For students...	**For staff...**
Planning to develop employability skills in a range of contexts	Engaging students if the work is non credit bearing
Prioritising reflection on their preparation for and part-time work	Finding the time to customise the PDS to our sport courses to increase the relevance for students and staff
Learning to articulate with sound evidence the skills they have developed	The engagement of staff who do not value the work

Enablers that helped practice to work

❏ Having dedicated timetable time to initiate the intervention was an advantage (year 2 *Preparation for Placement* module).

❏ Having a comprehensive university PDS to utilise for the intervention.

Points of advice

❏ Ideally you need at least one member of staff who has experience in the industry and has good relationships with employers to champion employability on your courses.

❏ Consider embedding the intervention in a credit-bearing module.

Possible improvements/enhancers

❏ Make the completion of the work either credit-bearing or an essential criterion for progression to placement or next year of course (Pass/Fail).

❏ Require students on placement to engage in updating their skills audit as they progress through their year's work – as opposed to making it a task to be completed at the end. Build this task into the assessment of placement through the placement portfolio.

The development of an enhanced understanding of employability

This case study indicates that students appear to have increased their understanding of employability skills and are more aware of those skills they perceive as important to their future employment. In the evaluation, students agreed or strongly agreed that the presentations and workshop sessions enhanced their understanding of employability skills. Likewise a review of the generic skills audits revealed that following the intervention students were able to provide appropriate evidence for most employability skills, despite somewhat elevated assessments of their own skill level.

Conclusion

The requirement for HEIs to engage in PDP facilitates an opportunity for this case study to be replicated in other HEIs. The PDS design may differ from one institution to the next but it is likely that all systems will have accommodated opportunities for students to address employability skills in preparation for employment.

The University of Ulster measures the use of the PDS across all courses in all faculties in the university. The centre of the university supplies subject teams with statistical evidence on the number of times students on each course have logged onto the system. The annual subject monitoring process, a quality assurance mechanism used across the university to monitor standards in course provision, delivery, development and administration, requires subject teams to justify their position and outline plans for improvements if the system has not been used to advantage. This is a useful mechanism to ensure that course/subject teams address the area of PDP. Ultimately the value attached to enhancing students' opportunities for developing employability skills will determine the degree to which schools, departments and faculties will engage the PDS resource.

References

Department for Education and Skills (2003) The Future of Higher Education

Department for Education and Skills (2003) Work-related Learning Report

Hind, D. and Moss, S. (2005) *Employability Skills*. Sunderland: Business Education Publishers

Little, B. and Harvey, L. (2006) *Learning through work placements and beyond*. A report for HECSU and the Higher Education Academy's Work Placements Organisation Forum

Appendix Summary and Evaluation of Students' Generic Skills Audit

A total of 32 students (f=15, m=17) completed the Generic Skills Audit out of the 100 who were given the opportunity to participate. The findings are presented for each of the six employability skill areas covered by the audit.

Communication

In the area of communication the students rated themselves with a fairly high level of competency with a mean rating of 3.62 (out of 5) and a modal score of 4. For all of the communication skills the evidence provided related predominantly to experiences within university life, sports teams and part-time jobs. Results of GCSE, A level and university assessment were frequently referred to as evidence of competency. These were mostly cited as self-explanatory evidence e.g. having passed all university modules the student felt that they had reached adequate understanding and knowledge of how to write well.

For skill one (ability to express oneself well in writing) four students attached work as evidence of their writing skills, however they did not provide the mark awarded for the work. This was a recurring theme, particularly in this section. Students were aware of the evidence required but did not provide sufficient depth of evidence to warrant the numerical score selected. Another example of this was citing job interviews as a means of evidencing experience in communication, but not stating whether or not they had been successful at the interviews or had received positive feedback on their interview performance. Lack of evidence was again displayed through wholly subjective statements, e.g. 'I think I'm a good listener' offered as 'evidence'.

The high scoring in this section might be expected if students interpreted communication in relation to everyday social interaction. Therefore, even if they find it hard to provide evidence in this section, it is unlikely that they will identify themselves as underdeveloped in the area if communication as they may assume that this would be an admission of weak social skills. Notwithstanding this point, two respondents to skill one (ability to express oneself well in writing) indicated they would like help to improve on this skill and seven students reported on their ability to match body language to what is being said verbally (skill five) needs to be improved. Skill five was perceived as the hardest to evidence in this section as five students did not provide any evidence even though three of these five gave themselves a score of 4 for this skill.

Amongst the female students (n=15) there was a tendency to describe qualities a person must have in order to be competent in that skill area, but they did not evidence their own experiences. For example, a student response to skill four (ability to attend to others views and ideas and understand their point of view) was:

> this skill is complex in that you have some form of knowledge of the individual...it requires the ability of being responsive and as I have found the key to success is gaining common understanding or negotiation of views, as it is uncommon for two individual's views to clash.

In this section the numerical scoring may have been quite accurate in terms of the students' actual level of competency. However, the evidence provided did not always reflect their apparent capabilities and often lacked sufficient depth. The ability to network easily with others (skill two) was the best-evidenced skill and was recorded as the skill in which the students overall felt most competent. The ability to match body language with what is being said verbally was the least-evidenced skill. The average mean for this skill was raised because of the wide range of scores. No other skill in this section displayed such a wide range. The evidential responses to this skill ranged more than others within this section, suggesting people were less sure of how to evidence this.

Working with others

This section scored the second highest average mean overall (3.72) and was rated the top average mean for female students with all the students considering themselves competent in this area. The overall mode of 4 suggests that the students have a substantial knowledge of the skill and are able to provide clear evidence to support their claims. The standard answers included being a member of a sports team, a coach, a captain of a team, group work in university, and part-time jobs. Similar to the communications section, students often provided evidence which lacked depth, e.g. saying you were a member of a sports team was sufficient to warrant a 4/5 for ability to work within a team. Again the high numerical rating may be a true representation of the students' skills in this area, but the evidence does not reflect the scores given.

Within this area all the skills had at least one student who did not provide any evidence. In particular skills three and six both had six students not providing any written evidence. Students documented positions in sports and other committees, such as the treasurer, in which planning is needed over a specific period of time i.e. throughout the sports season. As many of the respondents are involved in sports teams the need for time management was highlighted so that sporting commitments, university work and part-time jobs could all be successfully balanced. However, the mode score of 4 for this question may still be too generous for the overall depth of evidence provided.

Application of number

This area scored lowest in the overall average mean of 3.17. Evidence of numeracy consisted mainly of GCSE and A-level subjects, as well as successful completion of the information management module at degree level. The treasurer position within sports clubs was also documented as evidence in this area. The students did not appear to understand what descriptive and inferential statistics were and this is evident by the failure of twelve of the respondents to provide any evidence for skill three (ability to interpret inferential statistics). The responses of the remaining 20 students showed that they were unclear about this form of statistical work. Subsequently seven people indicated that statistics is an area which they would like to improve.

In this area the full range of scores were used (1–5), demonstrating that there are different perceptions of ability and competency amongst the respondents. This may reflect the widespread and well-documented belief by some students that they are 'not good at maths'. Despite being the lowest area of competency identified by the students, the scores were still at times over-rated, especially within the statistical questions as the answers reflected an overall lack of knowledge in this area.

Information technology

The information technology section scored highest in the average means for each area (3.91). The modes for each question were all either 4 or 5. This is the only section where the male students' average mean and mode was greater than the female students. Within this section the questions asked allowed for more objective answers and this was reflected in the scoring. For example question seven (the ability to send and receive emails) had a mean of 4.28 and the answers indicated that the students felt they were either competent at this skill or they were not and this was subsequently reflected in the evidence provided.

Typical evidence provided included the use of information technology in order to complete coursework, devise CVs and letters and design posters for events. Everyday usage was also provided as evidence for competency, such as being able to download music and videos, sending photographs via email, booking flights online and being able to shop online. This day-to-day usage of computers, alongside the completion of A-level ICT modules and the information management module, provides adequate evidence to support the relatively high scoring of students. As with previous sections however, more detailed evidence needed to be provided to substantiate their high competency score.

Despite having the highest overall area mean, the lowest recorded mean for any question throughout the entire questionnaire was in the IT section. The students did not feel confident about their ability to retrieve information from a database or creating a database (skill four: mean score 2.93 and skill five: mean score 3.03). For these two questions there were 17 responses that were left blank and 12 people indicated that this was the area in which they would like to improve. The scores were particularly low amongst the female students and suggest lack of competence in the construction and use of databases.

In this section ratings were somewhat polarised with students either rating themselves as good at the skill or not, but this may have been because of the nature of the skill statements. For example skill 11 (ability to use a search engine) had an average mean of 4.53; this may have been because the students felt if they were able to use Google, then this was sufficient to prove they were very competent at this skill. If more detail is required (such as the ability to use the different functions within Google such as advanced search, Google scholar or images) this might have needed to be stipulated more clearly to allow greater differentiation of competence levels.

In sum, this section, despite citing very high scoring, displayed the most realistic matching of numerical ratings and evidence.

Problem-solving

The mean score in the problem-solving ratings was 3.37. In this section the evidence given often did not illustrate the skill that was being addressed. As with the communication section, the students tended to cite university work, coaching and part-time jobs as evidence, but did not detail how involvement with these activities displayed certain skills. Within all five skills in this section there were at least three responses left blank in each, indicating that the students found this area a difficult one to evidence. In skill five particularly (ability to initiate, take decisions and act resourcefully) the quality of evidence provided was poor. Students described instances in part-time jobs which they felt displayed this skill, such as stacking shelves if they were empty, but an employer would consider this as part of the student's job description rather than a demonstration of taking the initiative. This section was not indicated as one in which the students felt they could improve upon. The lowest scoring skill in this area (mean 3.13) 'the ability to generate new ideas or conceive existing ideas in a new way' may reflect the opportunities that students have had to generate new ideas at this stage in their university careers. Overall the numerical scoring in his section was poorly evidenced in the student responses.

Improving own learning and performance

In this final section the scores were slightly lower (mean 3.38). There were very few ratings of 5 and some instances where a score of 1 was given. The evidence again was quite standard amongst all the students with university work, ability to use the library and internet to research assignments, jobs and coaching being cited frequently. The last four questions all had between five and eight students not providing any evidence from their numerical rating, but there was no indication that any of the students felt this was an area in which they needed to improve. From the mean scores it would appear that the skills five and eight were those the students found they were the least competent in undertaking: ability to identify and reflect on own strengths and weaknesses, ability to learn from a range of situations and apply learning in a variety of contexts, ability to defend argument using logical and systematic thinking based on sound evidence and ability to reflect on and critique own performance.

As with the other sections the evidence overall lacked sufficient depth to justify the numerical ratings. A recurring theme has been that the more 'subjective' the question appears to be the harder the students find to answer it and provide appropriate evidence. This does not mean they rate themselves any lower numerically, but they fail to provide a detailed answer to support their scoring. For skill seven (ability to learn from a range of situations and apply learning in a variety of contexts) a large number of students answered that they planned to/perceived that they could apply things they have learnt in their university course to their placement. Although this would be a valid example of applying learning, the students are citing foresight rather than hindsight and thus could not claim to have competency in this skill on account of plans for the future. Across the range of students there was inconsistency in understanding what each numerical scoring meant as many students were giving the same evidence but providing very different scores.

Conclusions

It is our belief that the numerical scoring selected by the students was often too generous for the depth of evidence provided. The scale is such that a respondent could always provide a score of 3 to suggest they are average at the skill and would not consider themselves underdeveloped, but are aware there is room for improvement. Although the definition of terms within the scale was explained with examples by the researchers, their understanding does not appear to have been sound in all cases e.g. did students understand what 'routine context' and 'substantial evidence' mean?

Areas such as communication and improving own learning and performance are difficult to evidence as the skills are not measurable, whereas some of the other skills are easier to measure i.e. for creating and retrieving files, you either can or cannot undertake that particular skill. The repetition of appropriate evidence across a number of skill areas reinforces the interconnectedness of many work-based and general learning experiences but also perhaps indicates the narrowness of some students experience to date. Students were also inconsistent with their own scoring with the same evidence being used to evidence different numerical scores (e.g. within the IT section a student rated themselves 5 for passing information management course at university, but only rated themselves a 2 for another question even though they evidenced a grade A in GCSE maths). On the whole there was an inconsistency with an understanding of what the scale definitions mean. Students were giving the same evidence for particular questions, such as 'took an A level in a subject', but one student would score themselves at 2 and another at 5.

A weakness of the intervention may be that given the students were aware that this was an employability exercise they may have been less likely to provide a lower, and perhaps more accurate, numerical scoring.

The 32% response rate to this intervention provides evidence that a significant number of students will choose not to complete work if the work is not compulsory or more importantly if no formal assessment is attached to it. Attendance at the preparation for placement classes (held once a week for one hour) was very inconsistent with students citing no formal assessment as the main reason for non-attendance at classes. As a result of this project a mark of 10% has been allocated to the completion of preparation for placement class tasks (2006–07) one of which includes the generic skills audit.

The University of Ulster PD System is a very comprehensive personal development planning opportunity which provides students with a mechanism to goal-set and action-plan as well as reflect upon personal, academic and professional skills and qualities. It has the facility to allow course teams to input course specific skills onto the system. The latter may go some way to customising further the employability skills required in the sport and leisure industry. The inclusion of course-specific skills and the decision to formally assess this element of preparation for placement should encourage students to take the identification and development of employability skills more seriously.

Finally it is thought the provision of a range of examples of evidence to support each level of competence (1–5) on a range of employability skills in each category would go some way to assisting the student in identifying more clearly their level of competence and the activities they would have to undertake in order to improve their competence.

4

Enhancing employability through critical reflective learning

John Buswell and Angela Tomkins
University of Gloucestershire

This case study explores the process of critical storytelling as a means of developing students' reflective thinking skills as preparation for future employment

The ability to really understand one's own strengths and weaknesses and how to engage effectively in personal and career development is a vital competency in the modern, dynamic and rapidly shifting world of work. This case study addresses an important element of employability, and at the same time an increasingly significant challenge to higher education (Barnett, 2000; Jackson and Ward, 2004) which is to prepare students for the demands of a rapidly changing world. Such a philosophy recognises that it is not simply what students know which determines the requirements of employers, and the needs of society, but increasingly, the ability of students to acquire new knowledge and skills and to understand how they can best achieve this and develop an awareness and control of their own learning. Indeed, Edwards (2001: 8) suggests that:

> employers are not interested in seeing extensive documented outcomes, but they do wish to see for themselves how candidates think and behave in new situations.

This demands ability on the part of the student to reflect on their experiences and to learn from them, and this provides the focus for the intervention described here.

This case study explores the process of critical storytelling as a means of developing students' reflective thinking skills as preparation for future employment. It is concerned with how students reconstruct learning from critical incidents experienced in the workplace to extract new meanings and new learning in preparation for employment. The influences of peer support and mentoring in enhancing reflective learning are an important element of the intervention. Learning inventories also allow students to assess their strengths and weaknesses in relation to learning capabilities and emotional competence and their use is also described in this case study.

Objectives

The specific objectives of the case study are:

1   To develop 'a model of progression' in the level of students' reflective writing skills from Stage 1 through Stage 3 of the curriculum, enabling them to critically articulate what they learnt from their 12-month work experiences as preparation for employment.

2   To identify, develop and pilot a range of techniques to enable the development of more effective critical thinking and writing skills, using peer support and the critical storytelling process.

3   To trial and assess the use of learning inventories which enable students to better understand and to assess their learning in both cognitive and affective (emotional) domains.

Context

The context of the case study is the Department of Leisure, Tourism and Hospitality Management at the University of Gloucestershire, where students across a range of eight degree programmes undertake a 12-month paid industrial placement as part of their course (40 post-placement Level 2 students were involved in the case study, working with 16 Level 3 peer-mentoring students).

Learning and teaching practices were well established for preparing, supervising and debriefing students undertaking the industrial placement, but it was felt that even more could be done to utilise the learning from such rich experiences to develop critical thinking skills (especially 'meta-cognition' and lifelong learning capabilities 'meta-learning'). Metacognition can be regarded as the ability to think about one's own thinking while metalearning is the process of learning about one's own learning. Reflection is the key to this and also provides the means to deep learning in the range of experiences addressed by the case study. The more enthusiastic students tend to engage in some form of reflective thinking, but it is not an easy process for some others; the essence of our approach is to enhance the learning processes of the former and to encourage the more reluctant student to become more critical and reflective so that students are able to challenge assumptions and to consider alternative ways of doing things as part of a dialectical process.

Furthermore, learning how to learn (not quite as simplistic in the context of higher education as some observers might think) also implies changed behaviour, or transformative learning, arising out of both critical reflections and planned actions. The emphasis is on student learning in which students construct their own meaning of the knowledge they are acquiring and gradually build up awareness and understanding of themselves as learners. Indeed, as Bourner (2003: 267) points out 'developing students' capacity for reflective learning is part of developing their capacity to learn how to learn'.

Learning how to learn involves experiential learning and making sense of it, but an important factor in the intervention was also the use of learning inventories. Learning inventories are questionnaires which provide a diagnostic assessment of students' capabilities and approaches to learning, such as critical curiosity, creativity, learning relationships, self-management and self-awareness as self-assessment tools and to provide the concepts and language of reflective learning.

Three learning inventories were used in this case study: Effective Lifelong Learning Inventory (ELLI), the Emotional Competence Inventory (ECI-U) and the Temple Index of Functional Fluency (TIFF) (see Appendix 1 for a fuller description of each). The explanation of learning power and learning capabilities underpinning the inventories, and pointers to help address weaknesses, enhance the ability of the student to understand themselves as learners and to become more strategic. Indeed, Yorke suggests that 'students who achieve well are more often students who are aware of their own learning processes' (Yorke, 2004) and therein lies the crucial point of the intervention. There is a symbiotic relationship between critical reflective thinking and self-awareness (metacognition). The more critical the student is encouraged to be, the more self-aware they are likely to become; and greater self-awareness facilitates deeper learning.

It is, therefore, critical reflective thinking which leads to changed behaviour, as Moon confirms: 'Experience is not quite the same thing as learning from experience' (Moon, 2004: 105). The case study acknowledges that it is often critical incidents and other 'trigger points' which provide the richest experiences to learn from and that one of the keys to learning from these is through the use of critical storytelling or narrative enquiry.

Critical storytelling

There is increasing evidence that the use of narrative enquiry or storytelling is an important tool for encouraging reflective learning, especially from experiences linked closely to employability skills (Danto, 1985, Moon, 2004, Schon, 1983). Indeed McDury and Alterio provide a persuasive case for its use in experiential learning.

> When we tell stories and process them, using reflective dialogue, we create the possibility for change in ourselves and others. Our capacity to express ourselves through narrative forms not only enables us to reshape, reassess and reconstruct particular events, it allows us to learn from discussing our experiences with individuals who raise alternative views, suggest imaginative possibilities and ask stimulating questions. (McDury and Alterio, 2003: 38)

They point out how recalling and creating stories are part of learning, and suggest that stories engage all parts of the brain – an important prerequisite for deep learning. They also demonstrate how reflective learning through storytelling involves several stages:

❑ Inner discomfort or surprise, but a memorable experience
❑ Events examined in more detail
❑ Outcomes in which there is changed behaviour. (2003: 110–11).

Danto (1985) also argues that the fundamental structure of knowledge is narrative, which provides a way of making order and sense of complex forms of experience, especially in collaboration with others. Collaborative learning is also central to the interventions in the case study and Rosie (2000) suggests that if students are supported in examining alternatives and making informed decisions then their learning achieves a higher level.

Peer-supported learning

The case study therefore acknowledges the social context of learning, especially in the workplace. Another key dimension is the use of peer support from students. The idea of students helping each other to learn is a growing phenomenon (Garvey, 2004: 6). In the case study, this takes the form of peer support, the use of learning sets and, in some instances, the training of mentors to work with students in lower years. This clearly involves another important dimension, that of learning relationships, which are central to both learning and employability, and highlights the significance of emotions in experiential learning.

We also might wish to note that shared, collaborative learning involves learning relationships which are also essential to employability. Relationship management extends reflective learning beyond cognitive and even metacognitive processes into emotional conditions and the ability to articulate feelings as well as thought. Hinett (2003) suggests that helping students to tap into their emotions is also central to reflective practice, and in training our student mentors, we must be fully aware of this dimension.

Emotional competence and learning inventories

Goleman (1995) popularised the study of emotional intelligence and suggests that it comprises five elements:

❑ knowing one's emotions
❑ managing one's emotions
❑ motivation
❑ recognising emotions in others

❑ managing relationships skilfully.

The case study takes the view that reflections on experiential learning and the development of metacompetences are limited without attention to emotional intelligence, and especially the positive dimensions. Frederickson (2001) points to a strong relationship between factors such as curiosity, creativity, wider range of thoughts and attention and the process of learning itself, which she also suggests are characteristic of learning communities and therefore learning relationships. It has become clear to the case study that the development of the skills of critical reflection and reflexivity require not just the techniques of reflective writing like storytelling, but an understanding of the concepts and dimensions of learning; when they can be incorporated into self-assessed learning inventories, with further opportunities for feedback from peers and tutors, then the goal of self-managed learning becomes more realistic for all students, not just the more naturally motivated and critically curious of students.

Description

The intervention centres on students returning from a 12-month industrial placement in the hospitality, leisure, sport and tourism sector, although it can be viewed in the wider context of the progression from level 1 to the end of the course when students present themselves to employers and the wider community. The work in Levels 1 and 2 begins the process of reflective learning and gradually helping students to understand their self-identity and their ability to manage their own learning through techniques of reflective learning and self-assessment. It progresses into Level 3 when students extend their reflective learning and their ability to articulate what they have leant as the next section illustrates:

The 'model of progression'

Self-management (Level 1) gives students time-management skills and confidence in the academic and planning skills for coping with the transition into higher education and beginning to reflect on their performance in academic skills. The ability to be critically confident and to understand the concepts of learning and personal development planning shaped the intervention at this level. Students' values and attitudes were explored and their ELLI profile interpreted and reflected on. Peer support was provided by level-3 students who focused on the level-1 students' approaches to critical enquiry and writing.

Self-identity (Level 2), builds on the insights from Level 1 and the resulting action planning, identifying strengths and personal challenges, and begins to develop students' skills of reflective writing and peer support. Some work was conducted in learning sets and through level-3 students recounting their critical stories based on their placement experiences. Consequently, students are better prepared for the experiential learning of the placement through their enhanced self-identity and skills of reflection.

Self-authoring (Level 3) enables students not only to know and understand themselves (also through the use of the learning inventories, the ECI-U and TIFF) but also to have the ability to articulate their skills and competencies to the outside world.

The focus of the case study is on the progression from Levels 2 to 3 through the critical impact of the placement. For many years it has been recognised that students return from work placement with many rich and varied 'stories' about their experiences. These valuable stories, based on real-life industrial practice, owned and experienced by the individual, provide huge potential as vehicles for personal and professional development. The willingness of students to share their experiences with their peers and tutors has also been evident. This posed the question of how to make the most of these personal stories about work experience so that they could be used as 'trigger points' for enhancing skills in critical reflection and promoting self-empowerment. The value of work experience to personal and professional development is unquestionable.

This intervention builds on current practice within the Department of Leisure, Tourism and Hospitality Management which involves introducing the idea of reflective learning in a Level 1 study-skills module and, by way of pre-placement preparation, encourages students to develop their skills in critical reflection by collecting and working with 'critical incidents' identified throughout the work experience period. The intervention is centred around a post work experience module entitled, *Professional Practice and Career Development*, which is supported by a final year module entitled, *Mentoring in Practice*. Amongst other learning outcomes the module gives students:

❏ opportunity and time to critically reflect on the rich experiences provided by the placement
❏ opportunity to evaluate their own strengths and weaknesses
❏ opportunity to develop skills in collaborative learning
❏ opportunity to devise appropriate action plans for personal and career development.

The module tutors began with two key underpinning issues which were:

○ How to help students develop the skills of reflective learning in association with workplace experiences.
○ How to use the critical storytelling process and peer support to enhance

this learning and promote personal and professional development.

The intervention therefore comprised the following elements:

❑ developing tools and techniques of reflective writing and especially critical storytelling
❑ enhancing learning through peer support and mentoring
❑ identifying the concepts and language of learning inventories
❑ encouraging ownership, empowerment and self-regulation of learning on the part of the students.

The module incorporates each of the elements identified above. Primarily students were introduced to the core themes of the module and particularly to the significance of reflection in personal development and professional practice. At this early stage they undertook a workshop using Moon's *The Park – an exercise in reflective writing* which demonstrated, through an account of an incident in a park, the four stages of reflective writing moving from a purely descriptive account through to deep and self-critical reflection which questions personal beliefs and values. Students were then asked to identify their own critical incidents from work experience and to consider the opportunity to learn more about themselves from these incidents. To aid this activity they were introduced to the concept of learning sets and peer supported learning. Each learning set was required to undertake a series on 'meta-learning tasks'. These tasks began with a simple account of a critical incident which was in some way meaningful to them. Students were encouraged to think about the emotions they felt in that particular situation and how they might have had an impact on their behaviour. They were tasked with thinking and writing about situations which had challenged their professional skills, attitudes and knowledge. They also had to apply the stages of Moon's stages of reflective writing. It was not, however, envisaged that students would have the skills to reach the highest level of reflective writing at this stage of their studies.

As the module progressed students were introduced to the process of critical story telling and were provided with *A Guide to Writing Critical Stories* (Tomkins, 2007). After a brief introduction to the uses of critical story writing and the importance of stories as an everyday means of self expression the guide was structured to provide a series of tasks to be completed throughout the remainder of the module. The learning centred on reflective writing in relation to writing a critical story which could be presented in a mock interview situation. An important aspect of the learning design was the role of peer support provided by final year students in the *Mentoring in Practice*. The guide provided a mapping exercise which demonstrated the links between Moon's (1999) map of learning and McDrury and Alterio's (2002) model for learning through storytelling.

The process involved a series of stages.

1   Finding and developing a suitable story for a job interview (students were provided with a range of typical interview questions to help 'jump start' the process).

2   They were then required to write a brief outline of their story. They were encouraged to think about how they felt about certain aspects of their interview story and to include these feelings in their story.

3   The story was then shared with one of the mentoring students whose task was to help them think about the story from other perspectives (maybe from the perspective of an employer, a customer or a colleague) designed to help them become more critical in their stories.

4   Students were then asked to expand their story and present (articulate) it to their mentor in a subsequent class based interview scenario.

5   As a result of this exercise they were required to indicate improvements that they would make to the original story and to indicate why these improvements would be important to their own personal and professional development.

Evaluation

Evaluation methods were largely concerned with:

❏ Student perceptions of the value and impact of the interventions on their learning and their self-development through module evaluations and other feedback.

❏ Evidence of student achievement and learning in their assessed work.

❏ Staff perceptions of the impact on student learning and their engagement in the learning environments.

1   Student perceptions

More specifically, there were several common points arising from student evaluations:

Reflective learning

❏ Students acknowledged that it can be difficult to reflect on one's performance and strengths and weaknesses and it is beneficial to have to do it. One student noted 'it has forced me to do things that I have never previously done and this is beneficial in every way'.

❏ Barriers to effective learning and self-development were identified through reflections and the use of ELLI. In some cases confirming what students already felt, but in other cases drawing students' attention to key issues and needs.

❏ Students found 'critical incidents' 'very relevant for reflecting and relating to theory'.

❏ Students, in indicating personal insights from the storytelling intervention, used phrases which indicate greater awareness of themselves as learners such as 'improve...', 'know myself better', 'focus on key strengths and weaknesses' and 'analyse my reasons for actions'.

Peer support

❏ Peer support stimulated new ideas and students indicated the value of collaborative learning in providing different perspectives on their stories.

❏ Collaborative learning is valued as a means of building confidence, 'working with others not only provides an incentive to commit but also improves confidence'.

❏ Many students would have welcomed a longer period of mentoring support from final-year students to enable the development of relationships between peers and to enhance their reflective-learning skills.

Learning inventories (see Appendix 1)

ELLI (Effective Lifelong Learning Inventory)

Most students felt that ELLI highlighted their strong and less strong aspects as demonstrated by the learning profile, and many pointed to the areas which they were going to work on. Many felt that it provided a good overview of learning and prompted reflective learning (see www.enhancingemployability.org.uk for a full and comprehensive report)

Emotional Competence Inventory: University Edition II (ECI-U)

The responses from students were overwhelmingly positive about the inventory and how it helped them to perceive their identities, their strengths and weaknesses and their plans for self-development. The dimensions of the inventory appeared to resonate with students and the profiles. The comments of students in their response to the profile was very revealing and suggested that the inventory had caused many of them to think critically about themselves and their aspirations and their plans for self-development. A key element of the ECU-I is self-awareness, and the attempts to develop meaning from these reflections and, in some cases, to be quite self-critical in a constructive and candid way confirmed the view (Goleman) that emotional education can be cathartic and positive for the individual (see www.enhancingemployability.org.uk for a full and comprehensive report)

The Temple Index of Functional Fluency (TIFF)

This is a tool that also encourages self-awareness and understanding to enhance and promote emotional literacy, but is much more concerned with the ability to manage relationships. Its purpose was to enhance the mentoring skills of some level-3 students and its rationale is based on the premise that good peer support and mentoring occurs through emotional competence and effective learning relationships and the skill of the mentor in managing them. Evaluations from almost all students were overwhelmingly positive about TIFF and its feedback on emotional competence and self-awareness (see www.enhancingemployability.org.uk for a full report and student comments).

2   Evidence of student achievement and learning in their assessed work

There was a clear range in student performance in their written work but, overall, there were a number of encouraging features in relation to the impact of the intervention. Students were able to:

- ❏ Develop very critical approaches to reflective learning through critical storytelling and personal development and reference to learning theories.
- ❏ Provide evidence of transformative learning through many illustrative examples of double loop learning.
- ❏ Discuss self-empowerment in relation to planning a career in leisure, tourism or hospitality contexts with conviction.
- ❏ Evaluate personal strengths and weaknesses including a personal action plan and to generate some very meaningful responses to the learning inventories.
- ❏ Demonstrate some clear insights into their emotional competence.

3   Staff perceptions

The enthusiasm of students was particularly encouraging and the feedback from them and other students involved in storytelling and peer support and learning sets was extremely positive and encouraging. Work by students in aspects of PDP and demonstrating achievement and skills development provided evidence of a clear understanding of themselves and a clear articulation of what they have to offer prospective employers.

Discussion

Enablers that helped practice to work

Although the practice has involved a process of discovery and developmental work for the tutors involved, it was very much based on established work over a period of over 20 years in industrial placements including pre- and post-placement analysis modules. Students were very positive about their experiences, but it was felt that the depth of reflective learning could be extended a little more and the capacity of students to understand themselves and to articulate their achievements also refined.

Other factors that enabled the practice to work were:

- ❏ A supportive environment.

    The Head of Department was very supportive of the ideas and the philosophy

Benefits to end users

Perceived benefits	
For students...	**For staff...**
Greater understanding and self-awareness of themselves as learners	A more enquiring approach on the part of students creates a more rewarding teaching environment for tutors
Increased self-empowerment and the ability to manage and regulate their learning	Reflective processes and PDP provide substance and academic underpinning to the personal tutorial system
More likelihood of achieving transformative learning through double-loop learning (in which the learner goes beyond straight-forward incremental improvements of their knowledge and skills and begins to question and challenge previously held assumptions in order to change behaviour – in others words, transformative learning)	Increased understanding of learning power and the learning capabilities of ELLI for those involved (eight tutors were trained to advise students) helps direct the design of teaching, learning and assessment activities
Lifelong learning capabilities	
The employability skill of mentoring, for some	
Deep learning through critical reflections	
A positive impact on students' critical thinking skills in relation to their subject	
Issues/Challenges	
For students...	**For staff...**
Reflective learning can be an uncomfortable process for some students. The challenge is to make it a meaningful process and to encourage students to engage in it positively, perhaps through assessment (academic work) and self-assessment (performance and learning) in which the role of the learning inventories is highly significant	There can also be an uncomfortable process for staff, especially when students' reflections go beyond academic boundaries and raise implications for counselling and therapy work. Tutors need to be very clear where the line is and where students need to go, perhaps, for further counselling
Another challenge is in the setting up and facilitation of the mentor/mentee relationship. It needs to be carefully monitored with clear guidance to both parties	A further challenge, as with students, is to encourage staff to engage positively in reflective practice

behind the planned interventions. The case study also dovetailed with developments in the University including the work of the Centre of Excellence in Active Learning (CeAL) and the support of the Dean of Teaching and learning Development.

❏ The external advice provided by advisors: Jenny Moon (reflective practice); Bob Garvey (mentoring and peer support); Rob Ward (Evaluator); and Steve Outram (HE Academy Senior Advisor).

❏ The enthusiasm of tutors involved was also an important factor.

❏ Good links with professional bodies and employers.

Bourner (2003) provides a persuasive argument for assessing reflective thinking. He points to the legitimacy which assessment confers on learning, including recent developments in work-based learning and suggests that 'reflective learning will not achieve full legitimacy within the academy until the assessment of reflective learning is secure' (Bourner, 2003: 268). The case study firmly agrees with this view and the growing acknowledgement that it is assessment that drives student learning, even when it involves personal and career development.

Points of advice to the HE community

1   It is important to build-in the concepts and skills of reflective practice, professionalism and professional practice and personal development planning.

2   Identify clear attributes for the programme with emphases at each level to align with the programme's philosophy and learning outcomes.

3   Provide a variety of approaches to encourage students to find time and space to reflect and record appropriate experiences. You may wish to consider how students observe and record experiences (at the time and afterwards). Learning logs and diaries are a very common method and the recording of critical incidents and initial reflections provides a foundation for later critical reflections.

4   Examine with students (and staff) the process of developing the 'criticality' of reflective accounts over a period of time and through several stages. Jenny Moon's *Park* exercise (Moon, 2004) provides a very useful resource, with a case study of four levels of reflection from being almost wholly descriptive in the first to more critical and metacognitive in the fourth.

5   Use critical storytelling as a process to encourage students to develop the 'criticality' of their accounts by, for example, developing interview 'stories'.

6   It is important that students draw on both subject theory and theories of learning and reflective learning to enhance the 'criticality' of their work.

7   The principles and practices of mentoring and peer support also give students a

conceptual and professional foundation for this aspect of work.

8 Reflective learning is useless without any responses to it so an important element to build in is clear goal setting and action planning.

Possible improvements/enhancers for this case study

1 The approaches to critical storytelling and the peer support worked very well, but it was felt that the mentoring provided need to be in place for a longer period of time in order to maximize the benefits for both mentor and mentee.

2 More content on learning power and emotional competence would probably enhance the students' reflections and action planning.

3 It was suggested by the external evaluator that the involvement of volunteers in some of the work of the project might ignore the challenge of enhancing the learning of those students most reluctant to engage in reflective learning. The team acknowledges the point, although it is planned to involve all students from 2007–08.

Work will also continue to build on the interventions and their findings to date. Resources will be created in digital form out of examples of students' critical stories during the autumn of 2007, and there is scope, perhaps, to develop some case studies out of the rich data which this exercise has generated.

The development of an enhanced understanding of employability

The case study has addressed the employability agenda in three main ways.

First, it addresses lifelong learning capabilities which underpin the notion of employability. The ability of students to know and understand themselves, and the achievements, skills and the competencies they have developed enable them to more effectively articulate and demonstrate what they have to offer to employers and to wider society.

Second, the case study takes the perspective that employability and citizenship are inextricably linked and require the similar philosophies and capabilities including emotional competence and an understanding of personal and social values and beliefs.

Third, the work of the case study also embraces the key message of the Leitch Report (2006) about the need to work against the perceived dichotomy of academic and vocational programmes and to improve skills, particularly higher-order skills. Metalearning involves the student in reflecting on themselves, not in isolation but in relation to their subject and their studies, their experiential learning and the world around them including employers and the wider community.

Conclusion

The distinctiveness of this case study lies in its attempt to develop a progression in the capacity of students to be critically reflective and reflexive in relation to experiential learning. The case study actively promotes the principles of self-empowered and autonomous learning, but recognises that for many students it will only be effective when they work in a structured and supported learning environment which develops their self-reliance and self-awareness. Integral to this approach are the tools and techniques of reflective writing and peer support and the use of learning inventories to provide conceptual understanding of the properties of learning and the language with which to describe and articulate the learning which has taken place.

The methods and findings of the case study apply in particular to all programmes which contain industrial placements and formal volunteering opportunities, but may also have implications for programmes which, perhaps through PDP processes, encourage students to make sense of unmediated learning experiences such as their own part-time work and volunteering experiences.

References

Argyris, C. and Schon, D. (1996) *Organisational Learning 11: Theory, method and Practice.* Wokingham: Addison-Wesley

Barnett, R. (2000) Supercomplexity and the Curriculum. *Studies in Higher Education* **25** (3)

Biggs, J. (2003) *Teaching for Quality Learning at University*, 2nd edn. Maidenhead: SRHE and Open University Press

Boud, D., Cohen, R. and Walker, D. (1993) *Using Experience for Learning.* Buckingham: Open University Press

Bourner, T. (2003) Assessing reflective thinking. *Education and Training* **45** (5) pp 256–272

Burkill, S. and Yorke, J. (2007) *FDTL Phase 5: Collaborative Research Project Final Report.* HE Academy

Danto, A.C. (1985) *Narration and Knowledge.* New York: Columbia University Press

Edwards, G. (2001) Connecting PDP to Employer Needs and the World of Work. York: LTSN Generic Centre

Eraut, M (1994) Developing Professional Knowledge and Competence. London: Falmer Press

Frederickson, B (2001) The role of positive emotions in positive psychology: the broaden-and-build theory of emotion. *American Psychologist* **56** pp. 218–226

Garvey, B. (2004) The mentoring/counselling/coaching debate. Call a rose by any other name and perhaps it is a bramble? *Development and Learning in Organisations* 18 (2) pp. 6–8

Gray, D. (2001) A Briefing on Work-based Learning. LTSN Generic Centre Assessment Series **11** LTSN

Goleman, D. (1995) *Emotional Intelligence: Why it can matter more than IQ.* New York: Bantam Books

Hinett, K. (2003) Improving learning through reflection, parts I and II. ILTHE members' site, now www.hea.ac.uk/resources

Jackson, N. & Ward, R (2004) A fresh perspective on progress files – a way of representing complex learning and achievement in higher education. *Assessment and Evaluation in Higher Education* **29** (4)

Lave, J. & Wenger, E. (1991) *Situated learning: legitimate peripheral participation.* Cambridge: Cambridge University Press

Little, B. (2005) *Learning and Employability.* ESECT, The Higher Education Academy

McDury, J. & Alterio, M. (2003) *Learning through Storytelling in Higher Education: Using Reflection and Experience to Improve Learning* London: Kogan Page

Moon, J. (2004) *A Handbook of Reflective and Experiential Learning* London: Routledge Falmer

NCIHE (1997) *Higher Education in the Learning Society.* Report of the National Committee of Inquiry into Higher Education (the Dearing Report)

Raelin, J. (2000) *Work-Based Learning: The New Frontier of Management Development.* New Jersey: Prentice-Hall

Rosie, A. (2000) Deep learning: a dialectical approach drawing on tutor-led Web resources. *Active Learning in Higher Education* **1** (1) pp. 45–59

Schon, D. (1983) *The Reflective Practitioner: how professionals think in action.* Boston: Arena Publishing

Yorke, M. (2004) *Employability in higher education: what it is and what it is not.* York: LTSN Generic Centre and ESECT

Appendix 1   Descriptions of Learning Inventories

ELLI (Effective Lifelong Learning Inventory)

ELLI is a learning inventory and questionnaire devised by Professors Patricia Broadfoot and Guy Claxton at the University of Bristol to be used in schools. There is now a national project to adapt it for higher education with the University of Gloucestershire one of the 13 members and the first to pilot it in May 2007

The ELLI questionnaire is a learning experience in itself. By visually representing a learner's profile on a histogram it demonstrates areas of strength and areas for development in learning. It challenges learners to think about various aspects of learning including some that they may not have been aware of.

ELLI focuses on the concept of learning power and the seven learning capabilities which it comprises. They include important dimensions of learning:

❑ Critical curiosity
❑ Making meaning
❑ Creativity
❑ Changing
❑ Resilience
❑ Learning relationships
❑ Strategic awareness.

ECI-U (Emotional Competence Inventory-University Edition II)

The inventory has been developed by the Hay Group, based on Goleman's work on emotional intelligence. It is designed to be used by university students as a self-assessment tool, although some background to the topic and the contribution the inventory can make to understanding oneself is important (the workbook is very useful in this respect). The Emotional and Social Competency Inventory (ESCI) is described by the Hay Group as:

> the latest research-based 360 feedback tool. It describes 12 competencies that differentiate outstanding performers from average performers. We use it when coaching individuals, and in helping teams improve their effectiveness.

Students are introduced to the concept of emotional intelligence and receive the following documentation:

1   The ECI-U Self-assessment questionnaire
2   The ECI-U Workbook
3   The ECI-U Feedback questionnaire.

Before they complete the questionnaire, they are asked to read sections 1 and 2 in the Workbook to give them the background to the questionnaire and how it can help their learning and their awareness of their learning. They then complete the self-assessment questionnaire which contains 63 statements about specific attributes or dimensions of emotional competence in four clusters of dimensions. Students indicate how much they think each statement describes their behaviour. There is also an opportunity to give a feedback questionnaire to someone who knows them very well to offer an external view on the statements. Having plotted their profile, they are asked to turn to section 4 of the workbook and complete each of the 'discovery' sections. The ECI-U is specifically designed to enable students to become more critically reflective; more aware of their learning; more aware of their strengths and weaknesses; more resilient and positive about their learning and self-development; and clearer about their aspirations and plans for the future.

TIFF (Temple Index of Functional Fluency)

TIFF is a validated psychometric tool based on the functional fluency model. It takes the form of a self-report questionnaire that measures functional fluency. It does not measure abilities or 'type' people. Indeed, an important feature of TIFF is that it provides a profile unique to the person on that occasion, not just an allocation of a category to belong to. This fact enhances TIFF's potential as a potent tool for behavioural change.

The results provide a profile of a person's behavioural tendencies and habits, both negative and positive, in a variety of situations and relationships. Expert feedback offers explanations of the model, along with support and guidance for making use of the results. The insights gained from these discussions stimulate self-awareness and understanding, and encourage positive changes for increasing interpersonal effectiveness.

Motivation for change is promoted by the empathic and encouraging style of the whole exercise, which is accepting of the fact that no one is perfect, and that everyone has some human failings. The empathic style in which the tool is administered is important in providing the non-judgmental and positive atmosphere necessary for optimum outcomes. Further information on TIFF at http://www.functionalfluency.com/?About%20TIFF

5

Developing employability skills through employer engagement in Foundation degrees

Vicki Hingley *Hotel School City College Norwich*

This case study evaluates the development of employability skills for students on work-based Foundation degrees

This project was well-timed in that it occurred at the same time as the Hotel School at City College Norwich (CCN) was considering a major change in its academic offering. Specifically the case study enabled the author to evaluate the development of employability skills on the hospitality, tourism and leisure Foundation degrees at CCN. The duration of the research saw a major curriculum change in the school from a two-year Higher National Diplomas (HND) programme with a six-month work placement, to a two-year work-based Foundation degree, with enhanced emphasis on work-based learning (WBL) and developing employability skills. Employers, students and tutors were consulted on 'payback criteria', developed in a previous project, in an attempt to find a useful way of assessing interactions with industry.

Students were also surveyed separately using a self-completion questionnaire designed to evaluate the development of employability skills. The survey identified an increased emphasis on personal qualities of reflectiveness, emotional intelligence and critical analysis by the students. Other skills identified as being increasingly important were self-confidence, self-awareness, teamwork, negotiating and decision making. The research has helped inform the development of Foundation degree modules and, in particular, two work-based learning modules. This case study includes examples of teaching and learning materials and considers future developments in the way Foundation degrees will be operated within the Hotel School at CCN.

Objectives
The objectives of the case study were:

1　To investigate the perceived benefit of employer engagement in Foundation degrees at CCN.
2　To review the development of employability skills for students studying the Foundation degrees at CCN.
3　To develop course materials to enhance employability skills of students studying work-based learning Foundation degrees.

Context/rationale
Hotel school
The higher education (HE) section of the Hotel School at City College Norwich (CCN) has been delivering qualifications in Hospitality, Tourism and Leisure (HTL) Management for more than 25 years. Demand has been strong as, initially, limited places were available nationwide for this type of specialism. CCN was one of the first colleges in the UK to provide HNDs and degrees in travel and tourism management in the early 1990s. Recruitment was strong and it was not unusual for the Hotel School to receive hundreds of applications for the 40 places available on the HND in Travel and Tourism.

This success, together with the growth of the leisure sector during the same period, attracted competitors and more colleges offering similar and related qualifications. This, together with the introduction of tuition fees in 1997, led to a steady decline in enrolments with a low of 13 enrolments in 2003–04. To counter this downturn, measures were taken to reduce the HND from three years duration to two, incorporating a six-month as opposed to a one-year work placement. This action stopped the decline for a year or so but the underlying trend was still downwards.

The four-year BA (Hons) Hospitality Management programme which regularly recruited 30 students per year was finally closed after a steady decline in 2003. Government policy and funding formulas caused the college to focus its resources more on the 14-to-19 education agenda. The HE profile within the College went into decline and needed a new direction. The traditional student market was also changing in a number of ways. Demand was growing for more flexible and shorter courses which would allow for the continuation of full or part-time work while studying. It was becoming increasingly obvious that the traditional HE learner wanting a typical three-year undergraduate experience away from home would no longer form the Hotel School's key target market.

Foundation degrees
In 2004 CCN started to explore the delivery of flexible Foundation degrees in Arts (FdA). Foundation degrees were a government initiative launched in February

2000 as a new form of employment-focused learning. Foundation degrees (FdAs) are based on the US Community College model of 'associate degrees' and were widely seen as a solution to the need to both widen participation in HE and to 'up-skill' the workforce. In 2000, David Blunkett, then secretary of state for education, explained the rationale for the introduction of Foundation degrees thus:

> Foundation degrees will raise the value of vocational and technical qualifications making them an attractive first choice for many students. A two year route to a degree with high market value because of its focus on employability will offer a new option for people, both young and mature, who do not feel that a traditional, three year honours degree is right for them. (HEFCE, 2000)

The main characteristics of the FdAs are:

❏ Accessibility – in terms of entry level qualifications and experience
❏ Flexibility – in delivery and provision
❏ Partnership and collaboration involving employers, colleges, universities and students
❏ Work-based learning (WBL) is a distinctive feature of the qualification
❏ Articulated opportunities for progression to honours degrees.

This product was seen to provide the best viable alternative for CCN in the face of declining demand for both HNDs and bachelors degrees. The decision was given a further boost in 2006 with all HE provision at CCN being validated by the University of East Anglia. FdAs also addressed the increasingly important widening participation agenda. HE is still seen as predominantly a middle-class preserve, with less than 50% of people achieving level 3 qualifications progressing to HE, whereas amongst those with A levels there is a 90% progression rate (fdf, 2007: 6).

Foundation degrees have already had some impact. Key statistics state that a higher proportion of Foundation degree students are coming from traditionally low participation neighbourhoods (HEFCE, 2007). This is good news for CCN. Initial feedback from our own FdA students suggests that course features such as flexibility, earn-while-you-learn, academic value given to work-based leaning and shorter (two-year) delivery, all contributed to their decision to enrol.

In developing the FdA the teaching team at CCN were mindful of the QAA Foundation degree qualification benchmark (QAA, 2004: 5) which identifies their distinctive characteristics:

> The distinctiveness of Foundation degrees depends upon the integration of the following characteristics: employer involvement; accessibility; articulation and progression; flexibility; and partnership. While none of these attributes is unique to Foundation degrees, their clear and planned integration within a single award, underpinned by work-based learning, makes the award distinctive.

In addition to traditional business management subjects such as marketing, finance and people management, Foundation degrees contain core modules aimed at improving employability skills. Such modules have a strong emphasis on self-analysis and reflection and require support and guidance from the employer. For many years most honours degrees have given attention to 'employability' skills within their programmes of study (team-working, communication skills, problem-solving, etc) but the curriculum itself has been determined around subject knowledge defined within the academic community.

An overview of CCN Hotel School qualifications from 2003–10 can be found at Appendix 1.

Work-based Learning and Employer Engagement

WBL is a central feature of Foundation degrees. It is the single most important element which differentiates them from traditional degree courses. This view is shared by all stakeholders (i.e. colleges, students and employers). The *Foundation degree Forward* journal (Issue 11, April 2007) states that:

> Work-based learning was also regarded as a positive and distinctive feature by both employers and students and operates as a significant descriptor in defining what both groups meant by academic backbone or level of challenge. The workplace operates as a locus of knowledge production and not just short-term skills training.

It was clear to the programme development team at CCN that WBL would need to be something more than a traditional (sandwich) work placement. In the new FdAs at CCN, students are mostly working full or part-time in a local hospitality or tourism business. Concepts such as experiential learning, sustained reflection, real work problems and the interface between college and work provide exciting opportunities for a new form of teaching, learning and assessment (TLA) in higher education. It is these concepts that provided the course team with a framework for developing the WBL modules and the subsequent methods of assessment. Implicit within these ideals are high levels of interaction between the college, employer and the student. Employers need to be engaged in integrating academic and work-based learning.

Description

This case study drew upon research findings from a small action-research project designed to explore the concept of 'payback' in the Hotel School employer mentoring initiative (Graves-Morris *et al*, 2005). This research resulted in the identification and creation of a list of 36 payback criteria (see Appendix 2) which are, essentially, the perceived benefits of mentoring for each of the stakeholders (i.e. students, employers and tutors). The original intention for this case study was to use this list to inform the development of employer engagement in the new FdAs. For this case study stakeholders were asked to prioritise what benefits they could gain from engaging with each other through mentoring and other work-related learning activities (e.g. site visits to employers). This data was collected via focus group sessions and in-class activities and the research revealed six criteria that were important to all stakeholder groups alike (Table 1).

Table 1   Payback criteria shared by all stakeholders
           (Lecturers, students and employers)

Understand each other better
A catalyst that develops new ideas
People 'out there' are saying really positive things about the Hotel School
Opens doors
Learning new skills
Can draw on expertise and real life policy-documentation-data

This stage of the research confirmed the potential benefits of closer employer involvement for the student learning experience. Although the data was useful for evaluating the benefits of employer engagement and allowing us to incorporate this into course handbooks and promotional materials, it was more difficult to incorporate the payback criteria into the formal assessment of student learning. It was decided that more specific research into students' employability skills development would be useful for progressing the WBL module on the FdAs. The author was keen to evaluate students' understanding and development of employability using a self-completion questionnaire based on Yorke and Knight's 39 attributes (see Appendix 3). This questionnaire was administered at three points during the project (October 2005, May 2006 and April 2007). This data revealed interesting changes in students' perceptions of the importance of employability skills as they progressed through their course.

Evaluation

The aim of this case study was to evaluate the development of employability skills for students on work-based FdAs in the Hotel School at CCN. The focus groups carried out with students, employers and teaching staff addressed the first objective to investigate the perceived benefits of employer engagement in HTL courses. The second objective was evaluated using data from the student self-completion questionnaire administered at three points during the project. The third objective resulted in the development of course materials produced, in part, as a result of the intervention. Finally the case study suggests materials that could be developed for future use on the FdA programmes.

Objective one   To investigate the perceived benefit of employer engagement
One outcome of this research has been to identify benefits of employer engagement that are common to all stakeholders groups (see Appendix 2 and Table 1). The pay-back criteria have been especially useful in underpinning the development of the FdAs and in highlighting the benefits for stakeholders of employer involvement in TLA on courses on the Hotel School. This has been beneficial in promotional materials for the FdA courses and in attracting both students and employers to CCN.

Although it is difficult to use these criteria for formal assessment purposes (as was the original intention), they have proven useful as a checklist in explaining the benefits of employer-engagement activities and they have also informed the approach taken to the development of the WBL module on the FdAs. This stage of the study reconfirmed the difficulties in trying to measure tangible and intangible benefits of interactions with industry.

Objective two   To review the development of employability skills for students
The survey conducted with students over the case study period reveals that perceptions in the importance of specific employability skills had changed. Tables 2, 3 and

Table 2 Personal qualities

Ranking	Oct 2005 (n=36)		May 2006 (n=34)		April 2007 (n=34)		% change Oct 2005–April 2007
	Very imp %	Quite imp %	Very imp %	Quite imp %	Very imp %	Quite imp %	Very imp %
Self awareness	41.7	55.6	47.1	47.1	52	44	+10%
Self-confidence	61.1	36.1	44.1	52.9	69	29	+8%
Independence	52.8	36.1	55.9	32.4	55	29	+2%
Emotional intelligence	11.1	58.3	38.2	38.2	44	49	+33%
Adaptability	50	44.4	44.1	47.1	44	44	(-6%)
Stress tolerance	44.4	47.2	41.2	44.1	49	35	+4%
Initiative	58.3	38.9	58.8	29.4	61	29	+3%
Willingness to learn	58.3	30.6	55.9	26.5	41	52	(-17%)
Reflectiveness	25	47.2	29.4	47.1	41	38	+16%
Malleable self theory	16.⁻	41.⁻	20.6	52.9	21	55	+4%

4 summarise these changes in relation to 'personal qualities', 'core skills', and 'process skills'.

In terms of change, the biggest percentage-point increases in skills that students ranked as 'very important' were noted for emotional intelligence (+33% points); critical analysis and coping with ambiguity and complexity (+19% points each); political sensitivity (+17% points) and reflectiveness (+16% points). Other increases of 10 percentage points or more were also evident for teamwork, self-management and self-awareness. Students' engagement with academic coursework and trying to balance work and study time may account for some of these increases, and a significant increase in political sensitivity is an interesting finding. The presumed importance of reflection became more significant as the student progressed through their studies and is a core part of the FdAs particularly the WBL modules (see Appendices 4a and 4b).

A decrease in perceptions of certain employability skills is also noted for *creativity*, *oral presentation* and *global awareness*. Although it is difficult to make definitive statements about why this is based on numerical analysis alone, the course team may

Table 3 Core skills

Rankings	Oct 2005 (n=36)		May 2006 (n=34)		April 2007 (n=34)		% points change Oct 2005– April 2007
	Very imp %	Quite imp %	Very imp %	Quite imp %	Very imp %	Quite imp %	Very imp %
Reading effectiveness	13.9	66.7	11.8	61.8	23	55	+9%
Numeracy	16.7	47.2	14.7	64.7	21	44	+4%
Information retrieval	25	55.6	20.6	47.1	21	46	(−4%)
Language skills	16.7	25	11.8	29.4	15	29	(−2%)
Self management	33.3	61.1	32.4	50	44	38	+11%
Critical analysis	22.2	58.3	20.6	64.7	41	35	+19%
Creativity	50	36.1	17.6	38.2	18	52	(−32%)
Listening	47.2	41.7	26.5	55.9	41	29	(−6%)
Written communication	19.4	63.9	23.5	47.1	23	32	+4%
Oral presentation	41.7	50	29.4	35.3	18	58	(−24%)
Explaining	38.9	55.6	29.4	47.1	44	41	+5%
Global awareness	33.3	47.2	20.6	47.1	18	41	(−15%)

Table 4 Process Skills

Ranking	Oct 2005 (n=36)		May 2006 (n=34)		April 2007 (n=34)		% points change Oct 2005– April 2007
	Very imp %	Quite imp %	Very imp %	Quite imp %	Very imp %	Quite imp %	Very imp %
Computer literacy	25	63.9	23.5	47.1	32	35	+7%
Commercial awareness	44.4	38.9	20.6	52.9	23	52	(−21%)
Political sensitivity	5.6	55.6	14.7	47.1	23	46	+17%
Ability to work cross-culturally	25	50	20.6	47.1	32	32	+7%
Ethical sensitivity	30.6	41.7	14.7	47.1	29	44	(−2%)
Prioritising	44.4	44.4	38.2	44.1	46	41	+2%
Planning	61.1	33.3	35.3	44.1	55	29	+6%
Applying subject understanding	47.2	36.1	17.6	44.1	44	29	(−3%)
Acting morally	30.6	50	26.5	44.1	35	44	+4%
Coping with ambiguity and complexity	19.4	63.9	17.6	55.9	38	32	+19%
Problem-solving	36.1	58.3	29.4	47.1	41	44	+5%
Influencing	27.8	38.9	20.6	47.1	29	44	+1%
Arguing for and/or justifying a point of view or course of action	22.2	58.3	11.8	47.1	26	44	+4%
Resolving conflict	33.3	44.4	32.4	44.1	35	35	+2%
Decision making	52.8	41.7	44.1	35.3	46	44	(−7%)
Negotiating	52.8	33.3	35.3	47.1	46	38	(−7%)
Teamwork	61.1	36.1	52.9	26.5	72	18	+11%

want to consider if the drop in creativity and oral presentation is due to a lack of this requirement for coursework. Perhaps students realise that working in small local firms demands less need to be globally aware than they had originally envisaged.

Objective three To develop course materials to enhance employability skills of students studying work-based learning FdAs

The results identified by this research have been used in a number of ways to enhance the students' employability skills. The payback criteria identified (Appendix 2) have been incorporated into course documentation, such as course handbooks to explain the benefits of WBL and employer-mentor activities. The WBL assessments of levels 1 and 2 (see Appendices 4a & 4b) also illustrate the exploration of employability skills by students in the first and second year of study. Table 5 illustrates the good practice materials that have been developed and are currently used on the FdA programmes in the Hotel School, and also highlights those materials that need to be developed. The course team are considering that a 'memorandum of agreement' be drawn up between students, employers and teaching staff – rather like a formal learning contract. This would set out the expectations of all three partners with the aim of maximising the experience for all involved and working towards standardising WBL. Such a document can also be used to make the students more aware of the importance of and need for developing graduate employability skills; which can then feed into the professional development planning (PDP) process and the requirement to reflect on skills development.

Enablers that helped practice to work

Enthusiastic students and helpful staff have facilitated this work which is an essential part of the action research process. Curriculum changes required a closer look at employment skills, due to the curriculum agenda altering direction so graduates were ready for the world of work and supported in WBL.

The action research method was a useful tool for this project as it allowed for continuous review of the process of curriculum development and change. This was particularly helpful in the development of WBL modules within the Hotel School's FdA programmes. It also identified a full range of employability skills that required development which will progress through to the BA (Hons) programme. The review of the mentoring initiative also highlighted the difference in relationships

Table 5 Course employability skills materials current and planned

Course materials	Current	Planned – to be developed
Student course handbook	Outline role of mentor	Detailed role of mentor
Work-based learning modules	Assignment level 1 module (appendix 4a) Assignment level 2 module (appendix 4b)	
Memorandum of agreement	College generic document (draft)	Specific hotel school agreement
Management of work-based learning	College generic document (draft)	Specific hotel school agreement

Benefits to end users

Perceived benefits	
For students...	**For staff...**
Results from this study will help develop links with industry by agreeing criteria for mentor activities, thus agreeing and meeting the expectations of all stakeholders Receiving recognition for their interactions with industry Having a much better understanding of graduate employability skills that help to equip the student for the jobs market post graduation and thereafter	Helps to clarify the role/purpose of curriculum staff visits to industry Provides a specific set of criteria that can be used to evaluate the process. Helps to develop work-based learning The information produced can be used for a number of purposes, including advertising literature, as a starting point for the writing of a memorandum of agreement with employers, students and college
Issues/Challenges	
For students...	**For staff...**
There were issues concerning full-time students finding employment in the sector/pathway they were studying Also employer-mentors were not always available in the workplace to help support the student in their studies. Students often change jobs for any number of reasons	Curriculum changes resulted in a change in the role of mentors in the work place There was also less time to take students on visits to industry The focus was now on students working and applying this to their studies

between students and mentors, with some organisations being more supportive of the process than others. The more supportive organisations can be used by the college as examples to others of good practice. This is particularly important for parity of experience in students learning, and for those who are undertaking WBL qualifications in SMEs.

Points of advice

The dynamic nature of action research was essential to permit the continual review of the project, however the curriculum changes during the study required a very flexible approach to the research and the focus on mentoring widened to incorporate a broader range of employability skills.

It was a challenge to get stakeholders, especially employers, together for focus groups. Greater success was achieved if one sought the opinions of stakeholders already together for another purpose, for example employer-mentor meetings.

These findings have implications for HE programmes in HTL, as well as for HE in FE in general.

Time was a major resource required from the researcher during this study, conducted over a two-year period, which at times proved difficult. However, the action-research methodology did facilitate the inclusion of research into teaching, learning and assessment processes and also included the involvement of students in the process. It would have been beneficial to have had greater time to conduct the work in greater detail.

Possible improvements/enhancers

Employer engagement could be improved by greater involvement with stakeholders in deciding their aims and objectives for the relationship. This may also help to standardise the WBL experience, which currently has varying success depending on the company and personnel involved. It is thought that a detailed written agreement between stakeholders would help to develop the WBL module with greater effect, which would build yearly to support the curriculum and the success of FdAs. The next step would be to come up with a 'memorandum of agreement' between the student, the employer and the provider/college.

Concluding comments

This case study has enhanced tutor and student understanding of employability. Students' knowledge about, and understanding of, employability skills was increased and their assignment work for WBL modules indicates this. There was also some evidence to suggest that students' employment prospects were improved as a consequence of the intervention, with graduating students gaining good jobs with local employers.

Early indications are that employers also benefited by employing students as part of the FdA programme in terms of capitalising on their learning in the business through work-based assignments. Indications for the college are that relationships between the college and industry have been improved; students were more employable at the end of their courses and the curriculum was regarded as improved. Foundation degree philosophy requires a full understanding of employability skills and WBL is at the core of this qualification. The study has helped to enhance our understanding of this and embed it firmly in the curriculum.

This study was unique to the Hotel School at CCN. However, it does have transferability to other FdAs within CCN as we all operate within a rural community, with a high proportion of SMEs and lifestyle businesses. It also has applicability to similar courses in other colleges, especially 'HE in FE' providers. The challenges we faced (and continue to face) in developing the FdA programmes and the approaches we have taken to engaging employers and developing employability may be used as a template for other providers. WBL is a real challenge to get right and good practice can, and should, be shared across the sector.

References

Carr, W. and Kemmis, S. (1986) *Becoming Critical: A Teachers Guide to Action Research*. Victoria: Deakin University Press

Foundation Degree Forward (2007) Where are we now? *Forward* 11 2007 p. 6

Graves-Morris, R., Hingley, V., and Mazey, R (2005) To develop the Hotel School employer mentoring programme and concept of industry payback. www.theresearchcentre.co.uk/pubs.asp

HEFCE (2007) Foundation Degrees, key statistics 2001–02 to 2006-07. Available from: www.hefce.ac.uk/pubs/hefce/2007/07_03/

HEFCE (2007) Grant announcement for higher education 2007-08. Available from: www.hefce.ac.uk/news/hefce/2007/grant/letter.htm

HEFCE (2000) HEFCE invites proposals for development of Foundation degrees available from: http://www.hefce.ac.uk/News/HEFCE/2000/fdinv.htm

Longhurst, D. (2007) Foundation Degrees: policy developments. *Forward: the Foundation degree forward journal* 11 April 2007

QAA (2004) *Foundation degree qualification benchmark*. October 2004 QAA 00510/2004. Available from: http://www.qaa.ac.uk/reviews/foundationDegree/benchmark/FDQB.asp

Appendix 1   City College Norwich Hotel School Higher education programmes 2003–10

Year	Foundation degree Part time, 3 years†			Foundation degree Full time, 2 years¶			HND Full time, 2 years§		
03–04							Year 1		
04–05	Year 1						Year 2	Year 1	
05–06	Year 2	Year 1						Year 2	Year 1
06–07	Year 3	Year 2	Year 1	Year 1					Year 2
07–08		Year 3	Year 2	Year 2	Year 1				
08–09			Year 3		Year 2	Year 1			
09–10						Year 2			

Foundation degrees

† **Part time**	1 pathway, first cohort started in 2004	Hospitality management
¶ **Full time**	5 pathways first cohort started 2006	
	Hospitality management Licensed retail Culinary arts	
	Travel & tourism Leisure & events	
§ **HND**	2 pathways last cohort finished 2007	
	Hospitality Management Travel and tourism Management	

All pathways have articulated progression to BA(Hons) Hospitality, Tourism & Leisure management

Appendix 2   Complete list of payback criteria (Graves-Morris et al, 2005)

1   Retention of 'just one' person in college who then joins the industry
2   Attract young people to industry
3   Potential to recruit staff: part-time and full-time
4   Raise profile of the industry
5   Opens doors
6   Opportunity to follow students' progress and identify likely future employees
7   Opportunity to work to attract/retain identified future 'stars'
8   Knowledge of curriculum – short courses available for own staff development
9   Provide evidence to support budget spend
10 Consider whether to apply for job with mentor company
11 Learning new skills
12 To match theory and practice and curriculum delivery
13 Formally evaluating the relationship between hotel school and employer will point way to future improvement
14 Deliver units in real working environment
15 PR exposure – newspaper, TV, journal
16 Use of demonstration facilities in hotel school
17 Knowledge of more students as people over a longer period of time
18 Opportunity to develop mentor employee (junior manager) skills in a different setting and school staff
19 Professional update for hotel's own staff e.g. source of information
20 Experience the industry as it really is
21 Will provide an opportunity to compare a range of mentor activities and formulate own future plan of activity
22 Understand each other better
23 Provision of work experience
24 Families will use mentor companies as they help students
25 A free meal
26 Opportunity to become involved in development of a competition culture
27 Provides live case-study base
28 Can draw on expertise and real-life policy documentation and data.
29 A catalyst that develops new ideas
30 Looks good on CV
31 Develops a feeling that the mentor cares
32 Makes 'us' look good as we are the only ones doing it.
33 Formalises links across industry-college-schools

34 Recognition of involvement in accredited workload
35 People 'out there' are saying really positive things about the hotel school
36 Feeling of ownership with mentoring organisation.

Appendix 3
Aspects of employability (Yorke and Knight 2006)

A   Personal Qualities

1   Malleable self theory: belief that attributes (e.g. intelligence) are not fixed and can be developed
2   Self awareness: awareness of own strengths and weaknesses, aims and values
3   Self-confidence: confidence in dealing with the challenges in employment and life
4   Independence: ability to work without supervision
5   Emotional intelligence: sensitivity to others' emotions and the effects they can have
6   Adaptability: ability to respond positively to changing circumstances and new challenges
7   Stress tolerance: ability to retain effectiveness under pressure
8   Initiative: ability to take action unprompted
9   Willingness to learn: commitment to ongoing learning to meet the needs of employment and life
10 Reflectiveness: the disposition to reflect evaluatively on the performance of oneself and others.

B   Core Skills

11 Reading effectiveness: the recognition and retention of key points
12 Numeracy: ability to use numbers at an appropriate level of accuracy
13 Information retrieval: ability to access different information sources
14 Language skills: possession of more than a single language
15 Self-management: ability to work in an efficient and structured manner
16 Critical analysis: ability to 'deconstruct' a problem or situation
17 Creativity: ability to be original or inventive and to apply lateral thinking
18 Listening: focused attention in which key points are recognized
19 Written communication: clear reports, letters, etc., written specifically for the reader
20 Oral presentations: clear and confident presentation of information to a group
21 Explaining: orally and in writing
22 Global awareness: in terms of both cultures and economics.

C Process Skills

23 Computer literacy: ability to use a range of software

24 Commercial awareness: understanding of business issues and priorities

25 Political sensitivity: appreciates how organisations actually work and acts accordingly

26 Ability to work cross-culturally: both within and beyond UK

27 Ethical sensitivity: appreciates ethical aspects of employment and acts accordingly

28 Prioritising: ability to rank tasks according to importance

29 Planning: setting of achievable goals and structuring action

30 Applying subject understanding: use of disciplinary understanding from HE programme (e.g. marketing, finance, human resource management etc)

31 Acting morally: has a moral code and acts accordingly

32 Coping with ambiguity and complexity: ability to handle ambiguous and complex situations

33 Problem-solving: selection and use of appropriate methods to find solutions

34 Influencing: convincing others of the validity of one's point of view

35 Arguing for and/or justifying a point of view or a course of action

36 Resolving conflict: both intra-personally and in relationships with others

37 Decision making: choice of the best option from a range of alternatives

38 Negotiating: discussion to achieve mutually satisfactory resolution of contentious issues

39 Teamwork: can work constructively with others on a common task.

Source: Yorke, M. and Knight, P. T. (2006) *Embedding employability into the curriculum.* Learning and Employability Series One. York: HEA Enhancing Student Employability Co-ordination Team p 8

Appendix 4a   Extract from Level 1 WBL module for FdA courses
Module Title   Work-based Learning 1

Assignment Title Work-Based Learning Portfolio

Assessment of Learning Outcomes

The following Learning Outcomes* are assessed in this assignment:

Discuss and negotiate work to be undertaken with tutor/mentor

1 Identify and describe defining characteristics of the workplace, the work sector and the individual work role

2 Reflect on the links between learning and work place activities and support available from the work-based mentor

3 Identify transferable knowledge, skills and understanding and construct, implement and review regularly an appropriate action plan designed to address

individual skills deficits.

*The Learning Outcomes for the module/unit are specified in the approved Module Specification – (UEA courses) or the BTEC Unit specifications.

Assignment Instructions

Part A Self-assessment and Action Plan

(You must attend a minimum of 70% of your WBL tutorials in order to pass the module)

For this part of the WBL module you are required to carry out a range of self-assessment exercises in order to assess you own strengths and weaknesses. You will also be expected to engage with your workplace to determine tasks which will inform an action plan for WBL 1.

1 Produce an updated curriculum vitae
2 Complete the Belbin self-perception inventory
3 Complete the Honey and Mumford Learning styles questionnaire
4 Complete self assessment of personal and employability skills
5 Complete a personal SWOT analysis
6 Evaluate your results from 2, 3, 4 and 5 and write a reflective summary which clearly identifies your own strengths and weaknesses
7 Produce SMART personal objectives for the WBL module
8 Construct an action plan-mainly for the WBL period, but potentially looking further into the future.

NB Part A must be approved and signed off by your work-based learning tutor.

Part B Identify and describe your workplace, and your work within it and the work sector

Present an account of your organisation to include such things as:

❑ The purpose of the organisation, its mission statement, its customers
❑ The characteristics of the work sector
❑ The organisation's structure and culture
❑ Your role within the organisation
❑ The approach to management, leadership and management style
❑ How the major functions of marketing, human resource management, customer management, operations management and finance are carried out.
❑ Organisational communications systems
❑ The use of technology.

Part C Produce a reflective report which identifies your learning and personal development

Refer to your action plan, employer report, and self-assessments to reflect on your own learning and development during the work-based learning period.

❏ Identify the employability skills you have developed
❏ Identify new areas for development (to be taken forward into (WBL2)
❏ Reflect on the links between college based theory and the workplace
❏ Id identify areas for personal career development
❏ Update CV.

Appendix 4b Extract from Level 2 WBL module for FdA courses
Module Title　Work-based Learning 2
Assessment of Learning Outcomes

The following Learning Outcomes are assessed in this assignment

1   Discuss and negotiate the work to be undertaken with tutor/mentor
2   Construct and review regularly an appropriate action plan
3   Evaluate the impact of theoretical perspectives on workplace practice and demonstrate the influence of work place learning in the reflective appraisal of academic study
4   With reference to reflection &/or observation, evidence and evaluate the embedding of theory in practice.

Assignment Instructions

The aim of this module is to build on your learning and experiences gained in WBL
You should be seeking to further develop aspects such as:

❏ higher levels of graduate employability skills
❏ increasing your awareness of business management issues by completing a work-based project
❏ planning for future career development.

   You are required submit a report which documents your learning during the WBL period. The report should contain extensive appendices such as; reflective learning logs, weblogs, critical incident reports, employer appraisals, draft action plans, tutorial records and research material. The report should be divided into the four parts as follows:

Part 1   Proposal and Action Plan 20%

This initial part of report should contain the following:

❏ An introduction which explains your role and responsibilities within the organisation (if the organisation is different from WBL 1, provide a brief overview of the organisation in appendices)
❏ Your agreed personal objectives for this second period of work-based learning
❏ Outline proposals of your work-based project(s). Ideas for the project should be negotiated with your employer/mentor and agreed with your college tutor.

NB Part 1 must be approved and signed off by your work-based learning tutor.

Part 2   Work-Based Project 50%

As part of WBL you should carry out an in-depth work-based project(s) on a specific aspect/issue within your organisation. You should construct a detailed action plan which states the project objectives and how you plan to monitor your progress through the project. Below are some examples of recent areas of study:

Implementation of an in-house training programme

Implementation of a new menu or analysis of sales mix

An evaluation of customer care procedures

A review and evaluation of standard operating procedures

Motivation and incentivisation of staff

Environmental study and energy management

Food and beverage cost control analysis

Audit of facilities with regard to the DDA

A review of the staff handbook in the light of new legislation

Recruitment, selection and inducting new staff

A review of customer care policies

Implementation of a sales promotion campaign.

Part 3   Reflection On Learning and Personal Development (30% with Part 4)

In this section reflect on your personal journey over the past two years and provide a reflective account which should focus on factors such as:

❏ What personal strengths have you built upon and developed?

❏ What skills have been attained and/or developed. How did you do this?

❏ What personal weakness have you overcome? How has this occurred?

❏ Reflect on how education and work experience interrelate.

❏ Consider how your learning at college makes a contribution to employment.

❏ How did your knowledge and skills assist you and benefit your employer?

❏ Consider how your learning at work makes a contribution to college-based modular learning.

❏ Does your job role relate to your studies?

❏ From your personal perspective at the end of your second period of work experience, how has your learning and development shaped your future objectives, aspirations and plans?

Part 4   Oral Presentation

In this final section use your reflections in part 3 to help prepare a presentation based on the following scenario.

The scenario

You have been selected to attend an interview for a job that you applied for upon graduation. You are keen to impress the interview panel and want to prepare yourself for the kind of questions that the panel will ask. From talking to your tutor and to previous students, you feel fairly certain that the panel will ask the following types of questions:

1   What knowledge and skills you have gained from your Foundation degree, particularly from the work experience element?

2   How are the knowledge and skills that you have gained relevant to the job that you are applying for?

3   What evidence you can supply to demonstrate that you possess the appropriate knowledge and have acquired relevant skills?

Prepare yourself for this interview by drafting answers to the above questions.

Instruction for the presentation

Your presentation will be given to an audience consisting of your module tutor and fellow students. (The presentation will be recorded to provide evidence for internal verification.) It should last 10 minutes and be supported by a PowerPoint presentation. You must submit an electronic copy of this PowerPoint presentation to your tutor. In the presentation, show how you will answer the above questions. In other words, reveal what answers you will give to persuade the selection panel that you have gained the relevant knowledge and skills for the job. Appropriate business dress should be worn.

6

International hospitality students' development of employability skills in the placement module

Stephanie Jameson *Leeds Metropolitan University*

This case study explores employability skills development of postgraduate international hospitality management students in a rapidly changing programme context

This case study focused on international students on the MSc International Hospitality Management degree at Leeds Metropolitan University. It attempted to discover how employability skills could be developed in the placement module as part of the masters degree. The case study initially tried to discover if this placement experience was effective in encouraging and enabling international students to develop employability skills which are appropriate and specific to the international hospitality industry.

The data collection method used was a form of 'story telling'. This was highly qualitative in nature and relied on the student telling a 'story' about their experiences. There was limited intervention from the interviewer and the respondents were allowed to let their story unfold and unravel. This offered a richer, deeper, more meaningful encounter and provided a more detailed picture of the international student experience.

The data revealed that although the first cohort of MSc students was relatively highly qualified, they lacked practical experience in the hospitality industry. Therefore, it was decided that a series of workshops (the intervention) be developed which would help the students learn about the international hospitality industry. However, when the intervention was operationalised the following year, it was discovered that the second cohort of students had different backgrounds to the first. The majority of students in this second cohort already had work experience in the industry and they were familiar with many of the operational issues covered in the workshops. Consequently, it was decided that a different type of intervention was appropriate. After much discussion, the course team decided to alter the structure of the course and also to re-position the placement period. It was decided to replace the workshops on the hospitality industry with a module which focused on cross-cultural capability.

This is the first semester of the new course and time will tell if this intervention has enhanced MSc students' employability skills. This will be evaluated at the end of the first year of operation. This case study demonstrates the dynamic nature of curriculum design, the need to be flexible in programme development, and the importance of listening to students and using their feedback to ensure that the curriculum is fit for purpose.

Objectives

The objectives of this case study were:

1   To evaluate international MSc students' needs for employability skills development prior to them undertaking a work placement.
2   To develop a module to help international MSc students develop appropriate employability skills prior to placement.
3   To review the benefits of the intervention for developing MSc students' employability skills and to review the curriculum as appropriate.

Context/rationale

The Report of the National Committee of Inquiry into Higher Education, the Dearing Report (1997) made explicit the importance of education for employability and highlighted the value of key skills development and work experience in developing students' potential for employment. At a more specific level, work experience/placements have long been seen as desirable for developing graduate managers within the hospitality and tourism industry and for undergraduates the nurturing of their attitudes and skills by high-quality work experience has been considered essential (Litteljohn and Watson, 2004).

This project focuses on the placement experiences of masters students on an international hospitality course and the relationship with their placement experiences and their development of employability skills.

This project was informed by the work of Taylor (2003). The main issue with this first cohort of international students was that although they could be described as Taylor's 'elusive creatures' – 'the well-qualified, well-motivated, intelligent, energetic and mobile graduate with management potential' (2003: 150) – they severely lacked work experience in general and hospitality-specific employability skills in particular. As a consequence of this, they were not perceived as useful or valuable labour by the majority of hospitality managers who interviewed and subsequently employed them. Further, this perception was preventing them from starting employment and once in employment, improving on the job.

In summary, they were finished before they had started. This lack of experience in the industry prevented them from achieving suitable placements and once they had secured a placement position, they did not develop. In the words of Yorke and Knight (2007) these students were 'in employment' (i.e. they had a job) but they did not appear to posses the qualities that facilitate and enhance employment opportunities. These students wanted (and needed) to enhance their employability skills in order to develop their future careers but they were hampered by their lack of experience. Although the aim of employability is to produce 'employable' graduates, these postgraduates were almost unemployable at least as far as graduate/postgraduate type jobs were concerned. Harvey (2004) defines employability in its core sense as the acquisition of attributes (knowledge, skills and abilities) that make graduates more likely to be successful in their chosen occupations. Employability is viewed as being beyond solely getting a job with emphasis placed on learning and ability. These postgraduates were not acquiring these attributes which would be more likely to make them more successful and in fact were in Harvey's words, 'just getting a job'.

Overview of institutional context

The background to this case study needs to take account of the historical development of the masters degree in what was then called the School of Hospitality, Tourism and Events at Leeds Metropolitan University. Since then the University has been restructured and hospitality management is now part of the Leslie Silver International Faculty. At the inception of this project, the masters degree had been running successfully for 12 years and had changed quite significantly during this time. In its inception, it attracted mainly home students with a hospitality management background.

In recent years, the course has changed radically. The number of students has grown dramatically, and the student body is now extremely diverse in its nationality, ethnicity, age and educational background. Currently, the students are from a range of cultural and educational backgrounds and can be segmented into hospitality and non-hospitality backgrounds. There are some students who have no experience of the hospitality industry either educationally or experientially. The course team quickly realised that these students were struggling in their acquisition of knowledge and understanding of the hospitality industry when they embarked on the course and decided to treat this group of students as 'conversion' students. A module was written which ensured that students, who had no previous knowledge of hospitality, gained 900 hours experience in the industry. These students were also required to engage in a module entitled *The Hospitality Industry*. This placement experience and the hospitality industry module were designed to ensure that masters students would develop employability skills which would hopefully enhance their career prospects in the hospitality labour market. The 'placement experience' has been written about in general and more specifically in the hospitality and tourism context.

As Walmsley (2008) argues, although a number of studies focus on placements, many do not attempt a definition. Walmsley notes that Markusen (2003) suggests that as with many conceptualisations, these are provided on the grounds of purpose rather than conceptual clarity. However, Walmsley suggests that this pragmatic approach is understandable given that there appears to be a broad consensus as to what constitutes the core of a placement. The literature on placement on hospitality and tourism appears to agree that the placement is a period of work experience which is part of the formal educational programme. Kusluvan, Kusluvan and Eren (2003) suggest that the student work experience can also be known as industrial placement, industrial experience, cooperative education, supervised work experience, internship or the sandwich period. The term 'practicum' can also be used to describe the placement period. Walmsley (2008) cites Daresh (1990) who suggests that the placement is an opportunity to:

1   Apply knowledge and skills in a practical setting.
2   Progressively develop competencies through participation in a range of practical experiences.
3   Test their commitment to a career.
4   Gain insight into professional practice.
5   Evaluate progress and identify areas where further personal and professional development is needed.

As long ago as 1990, West and Jameson argued that placement objectives particular to hospitality students were:

1   To develop contacts with potential employers and to construct work experience profiles commensurate with the demands of future employers,
2   To identify career paths within hospitality businesses and related organisations

From a review of the literature, it appears that the placement period is much more than a period of skills acquisition. Walmsley's extensive and critical review of the literature suggests that the placement period can be a time for career exploration (West and Jameson, 1990), can act as a 'shop window' of the industry (Sherrel, 1987), can be a confrontation of one's own expectations with the reality of the workplace (Waryszak, 1999) and can be an encounter in and experience with the labour market. As far as the author is aware, none of the literature on hospitality/tourism placements examines postgraduate placement experience. It is also the case that research on the placement experience in hospitality/tourism does not specifically focus on the experiences of international students. The current research should contribute to an understanding of postgraduate, international students' placement experiences in hospitality management.

Rationale for change

The rationale for the first change to the programme (the delivery of a series of employability skills workshops) was influenced by the fact that most students on the MSc had not had the opportunity to develop employability skills in the international hospitality industry prior to joining the course. The educational background of the vast majority of these students was non-hospitality specific and in addition to this they lacked actual practical experience in the industry. In the interviews, students reported they felt overwhelmed when they were applying for a placement and they felt very ignorant when they started working in hospitality companies.

The rationale for the second change, which resulted in the repositioning of the placement to follow one year of academic study, arose as a direct result of the intervention of the initial change where it was discovered that the two cohorts of students had entirely different needs. The rationale for this relocation was to enable students to acquire more academic skills which would enhance their employability skills before they embarked on the placement period. It was also to allow them time to develop more confident English language skills before the placement experience. The third change which removed the hospitality industry module and replaced it with the *Cross-Cultural Awareness for Managers* module (appendix 1) was a direct result of the first change when it was realised that some students already had extensive experience of the operational aspects of the industry but lacked cross cultural capability skills.

Description

This was a relatively long-term project and we learnt (and changed our views) as we went along. The original intention was to introduce one intervention which was based on the results of data collected from MSc students' interviews and focus groups. What actually happened in reality was that it was necessary to introduce a total of three interventions which radically restructured the entire course. This was not predicted at the commencement of the project.

All of the students on the MSc were individually interviewed and took part in a focus group. The outcome of this preliminary research was a realisation that these students had very little experience of the international hospitality industry. These international students had no previous experience in the hospitality industry (some had no work experience in any industry) and really struggled to find placements. Evidence from the placement tutor and the students themselves suggest that their work experience was nil, their experience of the hospitality industry was non-existent and their shock of a different culture all militated against finding an appropriate placement. Once these students found a job they struggled with employability skills whilst performing on the job. A combination of these factors appeared to have reduced the likelihood that students were really achieving their potential during the (compulsory) placement period.

Intervention 1

The first intervention was a series of sessions introducing employability skills in the international hospitality industry immediately before the student embarked on work placement. Some of these sessions were informed by the impact of cultural differences and others were informed by the nature of the international hospitality industry. It is clear that many of our international students had no prior knowledge or experience of the international hospitality industry. Also many students felt that they were working at levels way below their capabilities due to their lack of employability skills and/or English language skills.

The core themes of the intervention focused on employability skills and cross-cultural capabilities. The intervention was delivered by a full-time member of staff and two part-time members of staff who had themselves successfully completed the masters course. These two part-time members of staff had extensive experience of the international hospitality industry at operational and managerial levels. The intervention was based on the results of the primary research conducted with the 2005–06 cohort. The students who had been part of the primary research (2005–06 cohort) were predominantly from non-hospitality backgrounds. The vast majority of them had non-hospitality qualifications and needed the masters degree as a 'conversion' course as a route into a career in the international hospitality industry.

The intervention was designed around these students' needs and aspirations. The tools which were developed focused mainly on food, beverage and accommodation in international hotels and restaurants. Workshops were designed which aimed to encourage students and staff to interact and we developed hypothetical scenarios of food, beverage and accommodation around the world in 24 hours. The aim was to encourage students to think about the differences in international hospitality provision and how different food and beverages and different service-delivery styles and customer expectations could affect the students' skills when working in international hotels and restaurants in different cultural contexts. Each meal was taken in turn and there was a discussion of types of food, types of beverage and service styles globally. The idea of this workshop was to encourage students to think about other cultures and other contexts and the impact this may have on their employability skills and their ability to make a smooth transition into and successfully complete their placement.

It became very clear early on in the workshop that the 2006–07 cohort of students had very different backgrounds to the cohort who participated in the primary research. This meant that the majority of this cohort was particularly well-versed in international hospitality operations. Most of this cohort had spent extensive periods actually working in international hotels in a variety of countries. When we asked for examples of food and beverage operations in different cultural contexts the students offered many examples which were based on their actual experiences in a variety of international hotels.

This led to a review of the intervention and to decide that it was inappropriate to 'teach' this particular cohort about international operational hospitality issues in such depth.

Intervention 2

We decided that Intervention 1 had not been successful, due to the change in the nature of the 2006–07 cohort. What was important for these students was the structure of the course and the position of the placement. We concluded that the placement was not the most effective part of the course in which to develop their employability skills. We met as a course team and discussed various options for re-positioning the placement period and changing the module *The Hospitality Industry*. After much debate we decided as a team to sandwich the placement between semester 2 teaching and the commencement of the dissertation.

This had the effect of lengthening the course to two calendar years from one, but it gave students the benefit of two semesters of learning prior to starting work placement, instead of the previous course model where they had only six weeks. The rationale for this was that students would no longer be 'launched' into the hospitality industry in England with only six weeks experience of living in the country. It was felt that students would be much more acclimatised to the culture and – in addition to this – their command of the English language should be more confident.

Intervention 3

The module *The Hospitality Industry* was removed from the course and a brand new module *Cross-Cultural Awareness for Managers* was designed and developed specifically for this course (Appendix 1). The course team felt that these changes would enable these students to develop their employability skills in a much more effective way. Apart from the issue of employability skills, the course team felt strongly that the students' academic skills would be enhanced with this new course structure. The staff involved included the MSc course leader and all of the course development and teaching team on the course. The students involved were all of the MSc students who were enrolled on the course over two academic years.

Evaluation

Students evaluated the first intervention as it was being delivered. This could be defined as 'accidental evaluation'! It was very clear that for this particular cohort of students (2006–07) the intervention would not work. As a result of this we had to go back to the drawing board. It will not be possible to evaluate the second intervention (the repositioning of placement) nor the third intervention (removal of the hospitality industry module and the introduction of the new cultural capability module), until they have run their course. Both of these initiatives started in September 2007. The second and third interventions will be evaluated at the end of the academic year. Although this case study has not yet yielded specific data on the employability skills development of postgraduate students, it does highlight strongly the importance of being flexible when developing programmes in a rapidly changing context. This programme development experience has emphasised the need to be open to change and the need to listen to students and take responsive account of their feedback in course design.

Discussion
Enablers that helped practice to work

The main enablers in this project were the project team. The team were the epitome of professionalism. They were with us every step of the way. I found the project director and project manager extremely motivating and helpful throughout the entire duration of the project. My colleagues at Leeds Metropolitan were also supportive and helpful. The students who participated in the project were generous in the time they gave and extremely useful in the insights they gave me to their employability skills.

Points of advice

It is difficult to give advice as every case will be different and every cohort of students will present different challenges. My only real advice would be to be ready for the unexpected and be willing to be flexible. I had not realised how fundamentally

Benefits to end users

Perceived benefits	
For students...	**For staff...**
The benefits to the students should be threefold:	Staff who 'place' students in the workplace should be more effective in matching students to organisations as students should be better equipped to enter into hospitality companies and should be more 'work ready'
As a result of repositioning of the placement period, students should be able to enter the hospitality industry with enhanced employability skills and a deeper level of cultural understanding. This should benefit them in at least two main ways:	Staff who teach the students should experience more mature and informed learners whose English language skills are much improved
❑ First of all it should enable students to gain better quality placement positions and secondly it should enhance their employability skills whilst on placement. This should eventually enable students to gain better jobs at a more senior level in the industry	
❑ As a result of a longer period of learning at university prior to placement, students should feel much more confident in their use of the English language and it is felt that their academic performance will also improve. This could be evaluated at the end of the first experimental period	
Students will also have much longer to find a placement. Originally 6 weeks, with the new structure this is now 33 weeks	
Issues/Challenges	
For students...	**For staff...**
Students may find it more challenging to engage in the academic work before placement	The challenge for placement staff is to find placements which last for ten months instead of the previous period of six months. There will also be a challenge of monitoring students for a longer period

different two cohorts of students on the same course in different years could be. My two cohorts differed dramatically in terms of their experience in the hospitality industry. I had assumed (wrongly) that students embarking on our masters degree had a non-hospitality background as this had been the case for the previous few years. The approach to my case study was built on this assumption. However, in the end, the interventions were more radical than at first anticipated, so I feel that this ultimately made the curriculum changes more worthwhile.

Possible improvements/enhancers

It is difficult to suggest how the interventions could be improved as it will take time for the restructuring of the course to bed down. The only way to evaluate this will be to conduct a longitudinal study starting with this year's cohort. It will take some time to see if the repositioning of the placement period was a beneficial intervention. The next step will be to conduct research with the current cohort of students before, during and after their new placement period and to establish if the revised position of the placement on the course has enhanced the students' employability skills.

The development of an enhanced understanding of employability

My own understanding of employability has been enhanced throughout this research. Every case study is unique, but the particular slant of this case study was the focus on international students many of whom had no practical experience of the international hospitality industry.

It is probably the case that almost every domestic student that we teach has some experience of working in the industry. Some have extensive experience and most nowadays work in conjunction with studying. The cohort for the first stage of this research had severely limited practical working experience. This posed a particular challenge as the subsequent cohort was relatively highly experienced.

This case could be useful to other institutions as many universities are recruiting increasing numbers of international students, many of whom wish to spend part of their course working in industry. The case study should also be useful to the hospitality industry as the restructured course should result in highly qualified postgraduates who have completed a one-year taught postgraduate MSc coupled with a further year of industry experience seeking employment.

References

Daresh, J. C. (1990) Learning by doing: Research on the Educational Administration Practicum. *Journal of Educational Administration* **28** (2) pp. 34–37

Dearing, R. (1997) *Report of the National Committee of Inquiry into Higher Education.* DfEE: London

Harvey, L. (2004). *On Employability.* The Higher Education Academy. Available from: http://www. heacademy.co.uk/embedded_object.asp?id=21673&filename=Harvey

Kusluvan, S. Kusluvan, Z. and Eren, D. (2003) Undergraduate Tourism Students Satisfaction with student work experience and its impact on their future career intentions: A Case Study. In Kusluvan, S. (ed.) *Managing Employee Attitudes and Behaviours in the Tourism and Hospitality Industry.* New York: Nova Science Publishers

Litteljohn, D. and Watson, S. (2004) Developing graduate managers for hospitality and tourism. *International Journal of Contemporary Hospitality Management* **16** (7) pp. 408–414

Markusen, A. (2003) Fuzzy Concepts, Scanty Evidence, Policy Distance: The Case for Rigour and Policy Relevance in Critical Regional Studies. *Regional Studies* **37** (6 & 7) pp. 701–717

Sherrel, S. (1987) Give us a chance. *Caterer and Hotelkeeper*

Taylor, S. (2003) *People Resourcing.* London: CIPD

Walmsley, A. J. (2008) The impact of Tourism SME Placements on career intentions (unpublished PhD Thesis)

Waryszak, R. (1999) Students expectations from their co-operative education placements in the hospitality industry: an international perspective. *Education and Training* **41** (1) pp. 33–40

West, A. J., and Jameson, S. (1990) Supervised Work Experience in Graduate Employment. *International Journal of Contemporary Hospitality Management* **2** (2) pp. 29–32

Yorke, M. and Knight, P. (2007). Evidence-informed pedagogy and the enhancement of student employability. *Teaching in Higher Education* **12** (2) pp. 157–170

Appendix 1
Cross-Cultural Awareness for Managers Module

Module Title: Cross Cultural Awareness for Managers		Module I.D. 30000	
Academic Year: 2007/2008		Level: M	Semester: 1 & 2
Course: PG and MSc International Hospitality Management			
Module Leader: Isabell Hodgson			Internal Examiners: Isabell Hodgson
Assessment Method	Weighting	Latest hand-in date	
Annotated Bibliography	25	1 November 2007	
Presentation	50	3 December 2007	
Reflective account	25	1 February 2008	

To develop an awareness of working and studying in a diverse cultural environment. This module will assist learners to develop study skills; career planning and development but particularly an in-depth understanding of culture and cultural diversity and implication to both themselves as learners and employees but also for organisations in the hospitality industry.

On completion of this and other modules the learners will complete a period of industrial training within the sector (or a related sector) that they are studying. In preparation for this, learners will conduct a skills audit of themselves and begin to develop a career plan which will be implemented in the work placement organisation.

On completion of this module the student should be able to:

❏ Critically evaluate and develop reflective practice on their current skill profile.
❏ Demonstrate progression in personal, academic and professional skill sets.
❏ Demonstrate greater awareness and understanding of cultural, ethical and moral issues within the hospitality industry.
❏ Demonstrate synthesis of ones own future development plans towards preparation for the global economy.

Key skills

The key skills that are developed by the students are:

❏ operational (developed)
❏ planning and management of learning (assessed)
❏ communication and presentation (assessed)
❏ interactive and group skills (assessed)
❏ managing tasks and problem-solving (developed)
❏ self-appraisal and reflection on practice (assessed)
❏ synthesis and creativity (assessed)
❏ employability (developed).

Teaching, learning and assessment strategy

The teaching, learning and assessment strategy is based on a student-centred approach. The student is seen as a major resource and their experience in the workplace will be integrated into this module and the programme.

A range of information and communication technologies will be used to reflect a diversity of learning styles. Peer interaction will facilitate cultural and contextual understanding and lead to the potential for idea generation, modification, development and implementation. A range of individual tutorial sessions either direct or indirect will be used to enhance and facilitate the individual learners development.

The module will make extensive use of cross-university resources, ECIS, Skills for Learning, Library facilities and X-Stream. Key concepts and ideas will de delivered through lecture/workshop sessions. A number of employability workbooks/workshops will be used for those students on the placement route. The placement provider will be a key learning environment for particular cohort groups.

What's this module about?
The theme of the Module

The module provides you with an understanding of the contemporary hospitality industry and the factors influencing personal and professional development in the industry. The workshops will provide valuable opportunities to learn from each other. Learners will become more aware of the differences between working practices in a variety of countries together with cultural variances in service encounters.

The concept is primarily around creating an awareness of the cultural influences both from a service concept but also from a personal perspective.

The workshop sessions which will accompany this module and be conducted prior to the work-based learning period, will explore what is meant by 'culture', 'professionalism', 'development' and 'practice'.

Each organisation is likely to be very different in structure, culture and in the way it develops and manages its workforce. This module allows you the opportunity to explore these issues, observe, question and research further. You should analyse one aspect of the operation within the organisation and discuss the strengths and weaknesses which you believe feature. Hopefully, you will then be able to recommend some improvements or suggest new initiatives which the organisation may consider.

The module will assist in the development of the following study skills and increase knowledge and self-awareness for employment in the global and international hospitality industry.

Study skills

Communication & Information Technology, critical thinking and creativity, analysis and synthesis.

Cultural, ethical and moral awareness

Understanding cultural diversity and rituals, Recognising ethical situations and morality.

Self-reflection

Self-awareness, self-management, time management, group processes, learning through reflection in practice and experience.

Preparation for employment

Identify skills values and talents, strengths and achievements. Preparing self for work by identifying skill requirement. Undertaking professional development.

Learning training agreements & progress files

Preparing learning agreements, reflective practice, development and evidence.

7

Embedding employability in postgraduate hospitality and tourism courses through work placement

Emma Martin and Scott McCabe *Sheffield Hallam University*

This case study focuses on the development and integration of a supervised work experience (SWE) placement into postgraduate programmes in hospitality and tourism.

Reflecting on the curriculum development process and research with students, this case study evaluates employability skills issues for postgraduate programmes in the tourism and hospitality subject areas. The research incorporated a range of data collection methods including focus groups, interviews and questionnaires with past, current and new postgraduate students. Data was gathered on students' perceptions of management skills required together with an analysis of their career aims and skills development. This case study evaluates the challenges and issues raised at institutional, programme and module level arising from the development and integration of SWE placement programmes at postgraduate level with a specific focus on employability skills. Whilst there is a great deal of research on these issues at undergraduate level, this case study extends the debates into the postgraduate arena. The case study highlights the distinctive implications for industry, student support systems and programme managers and tutors and examines the character of demand for these courses (from largely international students) as well as outlining lessons learned from engaging in the development process.

Objectives
The project has three core aims:

1   To explore employability skills/needs of postgraduate students of hospitality and tourism.
2   To follow the development of 'work placement' into postgraduate courses.
3   To review and evaluate how 'employability skills' relate to the curriculum through the design of a postgraduate module.

The objectives were operationalised in to the following research objectives:

1 Evaluate how skills developed for work experience placement can be better developed through the curriculum.
2 Identify students' perceptions of the skills required by the hospitality and tourism industry and their expectations for skills development during their programme of study.
3 Develop and evaluate a module entitled *Developing Your Management Skills*.

Context/rationale

Over the last 10 to 15 years, it has become increasingly apparent that the character and background of students enrolling on full-time postgraduate programmes in hospitality and tourism has changed. However, the core curriculum of masters programmes has altered very little in character, aims and purpose to reflect these changes. Increasing diversity of students' cultural backgrounds is apparent and a growing proportion now come from rapidly developing nations in the Asia-Pacific and African regions.

Also the levels of experience of those applying for masters programmes has changed, in that many students now continue their higher education directly from an undergraduate programme in their home country. Across the UK international student numbers in HE increased by over 60% from 2000–05 (UUK, 2005) and small scale research has shown that around 50% of postgraduate students on hospitality and tourism programmes have no prior work experience (McCabe and Martin, 2005). Therefore the range and levels of students' existing employability skills vary greatly.

With the graduate labour market becoming more complex and volatile, and the number of graduates expanding, the employability of postgraduate students (PGs) is becoming more important. Indeed, a report by Oxford University showed 43% of employers felt the main drawbacks to recruiting PGs was their lack of industrial and commercial experience (Oxford University Careers Service, 2003). Over the last three years we have noticed an upward trend in the demand from postgraduate students for periods of paid full-time work experience, often utilising the placement talks for undergraduate students during this time. Despite the fact that employment-related skills are significantly important in the design of curricula in the hospitality, leisure, sport and tourism fields, there appears to be little research available which addresses specifically the employability of postgraduate students.

Employability skills

Whist consensus exists amongst key stakeholder as to the importance of employability there is still debate as to how employability skills are best embedded within the curriculum (Nield and Graves, 2006). Key work defining employability skills from Knight and Yorke highlights employability to be:

> a set of achievements – skills, understandings and personal attributes – that make graduates more likely to gain employment and be successful in their chosen occupations, which benefit themselves, the community and the economy.

> (Knight and Yorke, 2003: 7)

Considering the aspects that make up employability, Yorke and Knight (2004) identify three areas: *Personal Qualities*, such as self-confidence, independence and stress tolerance; *Core Skills*, for example, numeracy, language skills and global awareness; and *Process Skills* such as problem-solving, team-working and applying subject understanding.

With a focus on employability skills, other research, such as that by Raybould and Wilkins (2005) exploring the undergraduate hospitality student and the wants of hospitality employers in Australia, has addressed the importance of these 'skills' to stakeholders such as industry, education and students alike. The majority of the 371 hospitality managers surveyed in Raybould and Wilkin's (2005) study considered that there was a need for 'graduates to have a range of generic interpersonal and human relations skills. Whilst technical skills were seen as comparatively unimportant' (Raybould and Wilkins, 2005: 205). Managers ranked interpersonal skills, problem-solving and self-management areas as the most important ones for graduates. Recently in the UK, work by Nield and Graves (2006) has assessed different stakeholder's perceptions of skills required by graduates for employability. Drawing on preliminary data from focus groups, their early research found that whilst all process skills were deemed to be equally important, certain core skills and personal qualities were considered to have greater significance (see table 1 below). Overall their results highlighted that self-confidence constitutes a key underpinning area for development to enhance employability.

Table 1   Employability skills: ranked in order of importance

Personal Qualities	Core Skills	Process Skills
Self-awareness	Self management	All 16 as important
Reflectiveness	Global awareness	
Independence		
Self-confidence		

Adapted from Nield and Graves (2006)

Transferable skills not related to specific subject knowledge have been highlighted in studies such as the Dearing Report (1997) as important areas for consideration in relation to employability. Indeed this has been reinforced by Harvey et al (1997) who identified that:

> The need for developing a range of personal and intellectual attributes beyond specific expertise in a disciplinary field is becoming increasingly important and is likely to be more pressing in the working world of the 21st Century.
>
> (Harvey et al, 1997: 5)

This research highlighted that employers require adaptive and flexible recruits who can rapidly integrate into the company and exhibit a range of interpersonal and social skills alongside their educational attainments.

Work experience and skills

Work experience (or internships) have long been seen as desirable for developing graduate managers within the hospitality and tourism industry, and for undergraduates the nurturing of their attitudes and skills by high quality work experience has been considered essential (see Litteljohn and Watson, 2004). The hospitality and tourism job market places a premium on practical experience and 'students see internships as a credible means to land that first job' (Collins, 2002a), with placement companies often offering full-time employment upon graduation.

In the undergraduate market this balance of academic and practical experience is seen as essential and, in a study by Collins (2002b), all three stakeholder groups – employers, current students and graduates – agreed that industrial training could be improved. Two studies on undergraduate placement have specifically looked at skill development of hospitality and tourism students (Busby, 2003 and Walo, 2001). In an eight-year longitudinal study Busby concluded that whilst knowledge of working processes was a critical component for students they reported increased levels of self-confidence along with skill acquisition in (1) interpersonal skills, (2) information technology and (3) communication skills. Walo's work supports this. Assessing students' perception of management competence before and after internship, there was empirical evidence to support claims that internship develops students' management competence. So what of the postgraduate market? With more students being pre-experience how important is work experience to their future employability and management competence?

Recent research within hospitality shows that less than 10% of full-time masters level courses include a period of work placement (Jameson and Walmsley, 2006) whereas at undergraduate level the figure is 73%. With students on our postgraduate courses demanding placement opportunities it is on this intervention that the case study focuses.

Description

The initial approach adopted was to use the Course Development Team (CDT) as a platform for developing ideas about the possible purposes, aims and scope of the intervention at this level. The development group consisted of the two academics (one tourism and one hospitality) together with other faculty academic staff responsible for work placements at undergraduate and HND level; the chair of the course development panel; the faculty quality manager; the faculty-supervised work placement (SWE) manager and the SWE administrators. These early discussions yielded a series of issues that highlighted the need to clearly identify the expectations of the student group coming onto the course at this level. The development team then articulated the initial aims of the programme. These were to:

1   Enable students to apply theoretical concepts and professional skills to practical situations likely to be encountered by managers in the hospitality and tourism industries.
2   Increase the employability of students upon completion of their course.
3   Offer students on the SWE mode the opportunity to further develop practical management skills by undertaking a work experience placement in the hospitality or tourism industry.

The employability intervention on the postgraduate courses was twofold. First, the development of two work experience routes; and secondly, the development of a module entitled *Developing your Management Skills* (15 M-level credits). Planning for the two new courses incorporating work experience routes, International Hospitality Management (IHM) and International Hospitality and Tourism Management (IHTM), commenced in October 2005 and the courses ran from September 2006. The new PG courses followed the same curriculum structure as the corresponding full-time routes; 4 x 15 credits at PG certificate and 4 x 15 credit at PG diploma level. However whereas the full-time option includes a 60-credit dissertation, the new work experience routes adopted a 45-credit dissertation together with the new 15-credit module.

In designing the new curriculum the CDT considered the following issues:

❏ The need for the new route to be commensurate with the full-time course to allow students to transfer if needed between routes.
❏ To accommodate students studying for the dissertation at the same time as undertaking full-time work placement.
❏ How to differentiate between UG and PG work placement.
❏ How to implement an assessment strategy in relation to the development of management skills through both the module and work placement.

The development team concluded that to accommodate any difficulties arising, a minimum of six-months work experience would be satisfactory, and a period of up to 18 months could be undertaken. The latter was to accommodate employers' management development programmes into which the student work placement may be embedded. It was anticipated that the standard university 48-week placement period would be the norm for most postgraduates.

For successful completion of the work experience route it was decided that students should:

❏ complete a minimum of six-months work experience
❏ undertake and pass a performance review, assessed by both the employer and university placement tutor
❏ successfully complete the assessment package of the *Developing Your Management Skills* module.

The following section describes the module in more depth.

The module *Developing Your Management Skills*

The module aims and learning outcomes were developed in light of the discussions undertaken through the development process in respect of the aims of the programme. The module particularly aimed to develop students' management skills by providing them with the opportunity to reflect on their personal and professional development within a hospitality and tourism business environment. Specifically the module aimed to:

❏ Prepare students for the competitive process of obtaining supervised work placement experience through the deployment of LTA strategies focusing on CV development, interviewing skills, and preparation for work.
❏ Develop students' understanding of employability skills focusing on communication, presentation and inter-personal skills, leadership and teamwork.
❏ Enable students to reflect on their own personal and professional development throughout the process of securing, undertaking and evaluating the work experience element of these courses.

These aims were translated into the following learning objectives of the module:
These learning objectives are written as follows:

By the end of the module you will be able to:

1   Critically evaluate the roles of management and analyse key management and leadership skills.
2   Critically evaluate the suitability of your own personality and skills to a management career within the hospitality and tourism industry.
3   Develop key skills in relation to future employability.
4   Write reports suitable for the professional environment.

Research strategy

In order to develop supervised work-experience courses at postgraduate level it was important to undertake research into students' backgrounds, expectations, career goals and the skills they identify as being most important for career success. While it is possible to discuss these results in the context of employers needs for skills at graduate level, ideally it would have been useful to also explore employer's needs for skills specifically amongst postgraduates. However, this was only possible at the anecdotal level.

Thus the final adopted research process included the following steps:

❏ A questionnaire survey with graduating students of the full-time IHTM/IHM courses (those who had undertaken a pilot work experience/placement but not undertaken the module) to assess their understanding of employability skills. This was undertaken in November 2006.

❏ A questionnaire survey with new cohort entrants onto the SWE course to assess their understanding of employability skills. This was undertaken in November 2006.

❏ A semi-structured interview with students who expressed a wish to transfer onto the SWE course. This was undertaken in October 2006. The purpose of this interview was to explore with potential student entrants onto the SWE course their degree backgrounds, the level and types of work experience achieved prior to entry onto the course, their perceptions of expectations of a period of supervised work experience, and reasons for wanting to study on the SWE courses.

❏ Two workshop discussions with students undertaking the initial sessions on the module. This was undertaken in November 2006. The purpose of this session was to explore students' perceptions about the skills they considered were important for industry managers together with the types of skills they wanted to develop through the module.

Specifically the project team wished to discover what skills graduating students (i.e. a cohort who had just completed their full-time studies prior to the new intervention) felt were important for career success compared to the skills identified by new incoming students onto the SWE programme.

In terms of the sample sizes for the individual components, the following numbers were obtained:

❏ 16 student pre-intervention questionnaires (2006 intake onto SWE routes).

❏ 7 Students who have graduated from the full-time programme.

❏ 40 semi-structured interviews with students who wished to transfer to the SWE route.

❏ 2 workshop sessions of approximately 15 people per group.

Working with fairly small sample sizes on postgraduate programmes and the evolutionary nature of this case study means that statistical analysis and comparative statistics on the results are not possible. Therefore results have focused upon content analysis. As such the results are presented as descriptive and indicative.

The results of the research are presented in three sections. The first section focuses on the backgrounds of incoming students onto the SWE courses and their expectations of the work-placement route. The second section concerns the students' perceptions of the skills required by the hospitality and tourism industries. The final section looks at the aspects of employability and the skills that students saw as important for future career success.

Section 1 Student backgrounds and expectations

This data is derived from a set of semi-structured interviews with students who initially enrolled onto the full-time routes and then requested a transfer onto the new SWE routes in the September 2006 intake. This consisted of a total of 40 interviews.

Table 2 shows that 43% of these students had a hospitality and/or tourism related undergraduate degree and a further 23% had a related business and management undergraduate background. It is interesting to note that one third had no subject-related academic background.

Table 2 Educational background of PG students entering work-experience programmes

Undergraduate Course	Percentage of students
Hospitality or Tourism related	43%
Business Management related	23%
Other	34%

Table 3 also highlights that a total of 77% of this cohort had less than one year's work experience.

These data confirmed the initial rationale for developing the programmes in that

Table 3 Prior hospitality or tourism work experience

Time in work	Percentage of students
No prior work experience	32%
Less than 6 months	32%
6 Months to 1 year	13%
1 to 3 years	13%
Over 3 years	10%

they supported anecdotal evidence that the majority of students enrolling onto SHU IHTM/IHM courses were pre-experience and conversion students.

Table 4 reveals the results from a free-elicitation question asking students to identify the type of work they were ideally looking for from their period of SWE. A significant proportion seemed concerned less with the type of work than with the opportunity to gain some work experience in an international context as eight respondents stated 'any job in hospitality and tourism'. However, the majority of respondents identified that they were ideally seeking hotel-related hospitality work with nine respondents highlighting an international brand as being important.

Table 4 Ideal work-experience job

Type of work	Number of responses
Hotel	10
International brand	9
Management	5
Any job in H&T	8
Conference and Banqueting	1
F&B	6
Housekeeping	1
Travel agency	1

When asked to state the reasons for wanting to transfer onto the SWE routes, 58% of respondents identified that they wanted to gain experience (again the international nature of experience was also important).

Table 5 Reasons for transferring from full-time MSc to MSc work-experience route

Reason for transfer	Number of responses
Gain experience	14
Gain international experience	9
Enhance ability/skill	9
For career progression/employability	7
Gain confidence	1

Section 2   Student perception of skills

As part of the case study, students were asked to work in groups to discuss the skills they considered essential for working in the hospitality and tourism industries. The two focus group sessions came up with similar skills lists as can be seen in Table 6, with communication skills being considered a vital aspect for success.

Table 6 Essential skills for working in the hospitality and tourism industries

Group 1	Group 2
Leadership	Communication
Problem-solving	Project management
Communication	Personal development
Teamwork	
Managing people	
Listening	
Personal development	

Students were then asked to identify and prioritise those skills they themselves wanted to develop through the module and the SWE placement. It is interesting to note that no matter what the divergence of opinion across the two groups in relation to other aspects, when it comes to being asked to identify skills they want to develop and which they perceive to be relevant to their careers, they agree on the top four, namely: *communication skills*, *time management*, *stress management* and *how to motivate others*. Table 7 identifies the full list of results from the focus groups.

Table 7 Skills students identified as priorities for their own development

Group 1	Group 2
Communication	Communication
Time management	Time management
Stress management	Stress management
How to motivate others	How to motivate others
Delegation	Team building
Developing inner confidence	
Computer skills	
Problem-solving	

Section 3   Employability and future career success

This section reports on the findings of an employability questionnaire developed by Oxford Brookes University (Maher, 2004). This questionnaire was adapted for use with two groups of students. First, those students new to SHU (2006 intake) who were enrolled on the work experience courses, and secondly a small group of students from the 2005 full-time MSc programme intake who had not undertaken work placement and who were due to graduate in November 2006.

In response to the first main question; 'Which aspects of the content of your degree do you feel will be most important to you in your future career?', students identified the subjects in Table 8 as being most important (in rank order). While the 2006 group note that SWE will be important, the emphasis the earlier 2005 group place on 'work experience prior to the course' is interesting. Especially given that 64% (see table 3 above) do not have more than 6 months prior work experience. Other aspects that seem to be considered important are marketing, operations and the dissertation. Table 8 gives a more comprehensive picture of the results.

Table 8 Content of course you feel most important to future career (ranked)

Rank	2005 intake	Rank	2006 intake
1	Marketing	1	Supervised work experience
=2	Operations skills,	2	Operations skills
	Work experience prior to starting		
	course		
=4	Operations management	3	Marketing
	HRM		
6	Dissertation	4	Dissertation
=7	Finance	5	Work experience prior to starting
	IT		course
		6	Finance
		7	HRM

The questionnaire then went on to consider Yorke and Knight's (2004) 39 attributes of employability grouped under; personal qualities; core skills; and process skills. Students were asked to identify whether a skill was important using a five-point Likert Scale. The results in Tables 9 through 11 show each skill category separately followed by a discussion across all three aspects.

In terms of the *personal qualities* the two groups of postgraduate students identified self-confidence, adaptability, willingness to learn and self-awareness as the top four personal qualities for career success. Reflectiveness and independence appear much lower down the students' rankings. Table 9 presents a full list of the results.

Table 9 Students' ranking of personal qualities most important for career success

Rank	2005 Intake	Rank	2006 Intake
1	Self-confidence	1	Willingness to learn
2	Adaptability	=2	Self-confidence, Adaptability, Stress tolerance
=3	Self-awareness, Willingness to learn, Independence	5	Initiative
=6	Emotional intelligence, Initiative	6	Self-awareness
=8	Stress tolerance, Malleable self theory	=7	Independence, Reflectiveness, Malleable self theory
10	Reflectiveness	10	Emotional Intelligence

Core skills ranked by employers in Nield and Graves (2006) work identified 'self-management' and 'global awareness' as key whereas for our students these items were not considered the most important aspects of core skills. For the students, as can be seen in Table 10, critical analysis, oral presentations and language skills were much higher.

Table 10 Students' ranking of core skills most important for career success

Rank	2005 Intake	Rank	2006 Intake
=1	Oral presentations, Explaining, Critical analysis, Language skills	=1	Critical analysis, Listening
=5	Information retrieval, Creativity	2	Oral presentations
=7	Written communication, Global awareness	=3	Self-management, Global awareness
9	Listening	=5	Information retrieval, Written communication, Explaining
10	Numeracy	=8	Creativity, Language skills
		10	Numeracy

Lastly Table 11 outlines postgraduate students' ranking of *process skills* perceived most important for career success.

Table 11 Students' ranking of process skills most important for career success

Rank	2005 Intake	Rank	2006 Intake
=1	Teamwork, Planning, Problem-solving	1	Teamwork
=4	Resolving conflict, Decision-making, Commercial awareness, Negotiating, Prioritising	2	Problem-solving
=9	Coping with ambiguity and complexity, Arguing for/Justifying point/course of action, Computer literacy Ability to work cross-culturally, Applying subject knowledge	=3	Resolving conflict, decision making
=14	Influencing, Ethical sensitivity	5	Planning
15	Acting morally	=6	Ability to work cross-culturally, Prioritising, Applying subject knowledge, Acting morally
16	Political sensitivity	=11	Coping with ambiguity and complexity, Negotiating
		12	Commercial awareness
		13	Influencing
		14	Ethical sensitivity
		15	Arguing for/Justifying point/course of action
		16	Political sensitivity

Overall analysis across all 39 employability skills in Knight and Yorke's listing, the 2006 intake identified 'teamwork' as the skill they felt most important for future career success. The 2005 intake ranked 'self-confidence' as the most significant attribute and this relates to findings identified in the Nield and Graves study cited earlier. Whilst the findings from this study may not be identical to stakeholder perspectives in other research, both this study and the work by Nield and Graves highlights the importance attached to 'process skills' and their significance for career success.

Evaluation

Due to the sequence of course development, the roll out of the *Developing Your Management Skills* module, and the timing of this case study it is not possible to assess to what extent students feel the module, SWE placement experience and their taught masters programme actually contributed to their employability skills development. Students on the September 2006 intake are at the time of writing about to embark on their SWE placement. Early indications show that of the 15 placed students, 10 were placed in the UK, with a further five in the USA. All but one of these students were placed in hotels (the exception being a placement with a travel agency). It is reasonable to suggest that some students had therefore achieved their goal of an international placement in a hotel environment (the majority are overseas students and the UK is therefore classed as providing an international work experience).

In terms of perceptions of employability skills, it is clear that the students' views bear limited relation to those identified by stakeholders in the Nield and Graves study. The students' assessment of the skills required perhaps reflects their perceptions of the skills required to pass a postgraduate award as much as their future career as their most pressing and immediate concern. There is also the potential that their responses are influenced by the input provided on induction programmes and through the early input on the modules. There is little doubt however that this research with students will feed into the development of the *Developing Your Management Skills* module and the SWE placement programming.

The following section evaluates the main findings with a reflection on the process of the main intervention. It highlights key challenges and issues as well as benefits from the perspective of the institution, staff, and students.

Evaluation at the institutional level (Faculty)

The validation of the two new courses was a worthwhile process as there has been a strong demand for SWE from postgraduate students along with good applications to the two courses for the 2007 intake. Initial module evaluations show a high level of interest in, and benefits from, course content of the new module. Developing the course has also provided an additional incentive to strengthen relationships with employers and seek new and exciting opportunities for students elsewhere than the current employer portfolio. This has been aided by the additional investment from the faculty due to the demand for these courses. It is anticipated that these relationships will grow in the future offering increased opportunities, not only for students, but for employer and university cooperation.

The entire intervention has posed challenges throughout the year for administrative staff and placement officers, course leaders and the module team as well as students and their expectations. One of the key issues for the future success of the courses is the development of close working relationships and the joining up of functions across the existing organisational structures. There were clear differences between the levels of service required for the postgraduate students compared to their undergraduate counterparts. Placement office staff and employer liaison tutors identified the potential for challenges for employers in the following ways: some employers preferred undergraduate students on placements and did not want postgraduates; some employers had unrealistic expectations of postgraduates in that they did not fully understand the different (i.e. international, pre-experience, conversion) backgrounds of the cohort. Politically, postgraduate placements were seen to pose a potential threat to existing undergraduate placement demand in a challenging HE environment dominated by the higher tuition fees and the impacts this might hold for undergraduate placement provision/demand.

While the market for undergraduate placements may contract due to the increases in tuition fees and the demand for temporary part-time paid employment amongst the undergraduate student body, the development of a market for postgraduate SWE placements is a key opportunity. However, this requires a change in culture and practice at the institutional level and the ways in which it engages with its placement providers.

Throughout this process of evaluation three key issues emerged:

❏ The need to generate opportunities for postgraduate student placements through contact with, and education of, potential employers.

❏ Provision of appropriate support systems for postgraduate students wishing to undertake SWE placements.

❏ Managing expectations of all stakeholders (employers, students and staff [including overseas recruitment agents]) to ensure that expectations could be met by all concerned.

Evaluation at the programmes' level

Of the 40 original students interviewed and transferred onto the SWE courses, 16 did not engage with the recruitment and selection process associated with work placement (this does not mean that they did not engage with the module. This means that they failed to go to any employer presentations; they did not submit applications or CVs or any other activity provided in securing a work placement). As of 5 July 2007, 15 students had secured placements with a further nine students having applications outstanding.

In terms of operations and workload planning, an issue was identified in relation to the supervision of these students. At the time of the supervisor allocation, the students are enrolled on the 45-credit dissertation. However, due to a large number of students reverting back to the full-time route and the 60-credit version, there is a consequent impact on workloads for lecturing staff. The main issue is that those students opting for the work-experience route have the flexibility to complete their dissertation before, during or after their period of professional practice. In reality

Benefits to end users

Perceived benefits	
For students...	For staff...
Practical work experience in an international context	Greater connections made within the taught programme to the employability skills and industry context
Exposure to international working practices	
Development of language and communication skill	Closer working relationships with industry partners
Enhancement of networks within the chosen industry sector	Greater understanding of the employability issues surrounding postgraduate international students
Career enhancement based on skills and experience	Raises the profile of employability internally within the university/faculty
Exposure to, and development of, employability skills during taught module	Enhanced student demand through increased perceived relevance of the course to career development
Issues/Challenges	
For students...	For staff...
Attendance and engagement were required on a more professional level	Work loading issues due to student demand
	Delivery patterns
Engagement with the recruitment and selection process and time frame to which employers work	Managing expectations of all stakeholders
	Differentiation from undergraduate work placement
Completion of MSc and dissertation due to work opportunities	Generation of postgraduate placements
	Organisation and systems needed to run new employability/placement focus to postgraduate courses

this has created work-loading issues as students allocated supervisors in March 2007 have chosen not to engage in the dissertation process until January 2009. Tracking students through the dissertation process is an element the module team and administrators need to manage.

Evaluation at the module level

Whilst students benefited from the content of the *Developing Your Management Skills* module greatly, attendance and engagement in the latter part of the module was an issue. The possible reasons for this were explored with students picking up module assessment material missed through non-attendance. Issues arising were as follows:

- ❏ The delivery pattern of the taught element of the module was unsuitable at two five-week sessions across the autumn and spring semesters.
- ❏ Timetabling issues, part-time work and the lack of assessment during the taught period.

This highlights a potential problem associated with the instrumental, assessment-driven nature of HE provision impacting on attendance.

Discussion

We feel we have learned a great deal from participating in this employability intervention and from undertaking the research associated with this case study. Whilst not all students engaged with the module/work experience opportunities in the way that we would have wished, there are certainly lessons that have been learnt.

Enablers that helped practice to work

- ❏ Having the backing of the faculty to embed employability and work placement into the postgraduate programmes enabled development time and investment into a suitable strategy for the intervention.
- ❏ Key industry contacts supportive of the development of the intervention and significant numbers of placement opportunities with a diverse skill and cultural background.
- ❏ Interest and demand from students on full-time courses and feedback on the demand for these types of opportunities from key international recruitment agents.
- ❏ Engaged employers willing to offer placement for postgraduate students alongside undergraduate placement.
- ❏ The strength of personal networks of key academic members of staff and their ability to engage employers.
- ❏ Reputation of the programme both internally and across the sector.

Points of advice

As the first cohort has yet to graduate, it is difficult to give a lot of advice related to this intervention. The validation of the two new courses containing placement was a worthwhile process as there has been a real demand for SWE from postgraduate students although delivery of the intervention has presented challenges.

There needs to be a clear strategy to make explicit why employability and placement opportunities are to be embedded within postgraduate level courses. Faculty need to understand why they are embarking on this route. Likewise employers need to be fully briefed on the differences between traditional UK undergraduate students, and international postgraduate students, and they also need to show a clear commitment to the skills and development needs of the latter group. Subsequent expectation at all levels, from administrative staff and placement officers through to course leaders and the module team as well as students and employers need to be managed carefully.

Possible improvements/enhancers

After review and evaluation of the first year of the intervention the following were identified as areas to improve/enhance:

❑ Delivery patterns

First-year module delivery was based on two five-week blocks. This was changed for the second year to a full 12-week single 2nd semester pattern. This has enhanced attendance to the *Developing Your Management Skills* Module. This has also allowed the placement team and administrative staff to evaluate students' commitment to the placement process and transfer those not engaging back to the full-time route earlier than in the previous year.

❑ As the courses and intervention become embedded within the faculty, the involvement and integration of university student-support teams has been enhanced and should develop further over the next few years.

External/internal commentary

With the first cohort currently out on placement, employer commentary from the intervention is difficult to provide. However, informal feedback in comments from placement tutors and employers tells us the students are successful in the workplace and feedback through the programme committee and module evaluation is positive about the new module. Internally employability and placement at postgraduate level is increasing in importance within the faculty and other postgraduate courses are taking on board these developments (e.g. MSc HRM has now developed a work-based-learning module).

The development of an enhanced understanding of employability

This case study has enhanced the students' understanding of employability particularly in relation to a professional attitude to the skills required as distinct from academic skills. The diversity of employability, and the fact that it is dependent upon students' personal career aspirations, has also been highlighted. The *Developing Your Management Skills* module increased students' knowledge of the employability skills valued by industry and allowed them to compare this with their own perceptions of the relevant skills required for a successful career.

In terms of academic staff the emphasis placed on interpersonal and adaptability skills along with self-management by the tourism and hospitality industries has fed into taught programmes. The case study has also enabled greater networking and closer working relationships between academic and industry partners leading to opportunities for knowledge transfer.

References

Busby, G. (2003) Tourism degree internships: a longitudinal study. *Journal of Vocational Education and Training* **55** (3)

Collins A. (2002a) Gateway to the real world, industrial training: dilemmas and problems. *Tourism Management* **23** (1) pp. 93–96

Collins A. (2002b) Are We Teaching What We Should? Dilemmas and Problems in Tourism and Hotel Management Education. *Tourism Analysis* **7** (2) pp. 151–163

Dearing, R (1997) *Report of National Committee of Inquiry into Higher Education.* London: DfEE

Harvey, L. Moon, S. and Geall, V. (1997), *Graduates Work: Organisational Change and Students Attributes.* Birmingham: Centre for Research into Quality

Jameson, S. and Walmsley, A. (2006) *A Review of Hospitality Management Education in the UK 2006.* Council for Hospitality Management Education

Knight, P. and Yorke, M. (2003), *Assessment, Learning and Employability.* Maidenhead: Open University Press

Litteljohn, D. and Watson, S. (2004) Developing graduate managers for hospitality and tourism. *International Journal of Contemporary Hospitality Management* **16** (7) pp. 408–414

Maher, A. (2004). Oven-ready and self-basting? Taking stock of employability skills. *LINK* **11** Higher Education Academy Network for Hospitality, Leisure, Sport and Tourism pp. 7–9

McCabe, S. and Martin, E (2005) *Report on Postgraduate Students Employment and Study Patterns 2005.* Unpublished report Sheffield Hallam University

Nield, K. and Graves, S. (2006) *Enhancing Graduate Employability: Stakeholder Perspectives.* Paper presented at the Council for Hospitality Management Education Conference, Nottingham, May

Oxford University Careers Service (2003) *Survey of employer's views on the employability of Oxford postgraduate students and recruitment practices.* Available from: www.skillsportal.ox.ac.uk/documents/employer_suvey.pdf

Raybould, M. and Wilkins, H. (2005) Over Qualified and under Experienced: turning graduates into hospitality managers. *International Journal of Contemporary Hospitality Management* **17** (3) pp. 203–216

Univerisities UK. (2005) International Strategy. London. Universities UK

Walo, M. (2001) Assessing the contribution of internship in developing Australian tourism and hospitality students. *Asia Pacific Journal of Cooperative Education* **2** (1) pp. 12–28

Yorke. M, and Knight, P. (2004) *Learning, Curriculum and Employability in Higher Education.* London: Routledge Falmer

8

Enhancing employability through work-based assessment

Conor Sheehan and Linda Waghorn
Westminster Kingsway College

This case study examines the use of problem-based assessment, applied in a workplace setting, to enhance students' employability

This case study examines the feasibility of developing problem-based assessment in the workplace for Hospitality Management Foundation Arts degree (FdA) students. The primary aim of this initiative was to enhance graduate employability by offering a broader and more realistic framework for the assessment of skills, knowledge and analytical ability. One of the central questions underpinning this research focused on identifying which types of employer involvement are appropriate and most effective in the development of work-based assessment programmes. Given the vocational nature of Foundation degrees it is generally expected that employers will be involved with both their planning and validation. The authors felt that developing closer relationships with employers by having them more closely involved in the design and assessment of student learning (i.e. their assignments) would be beneficial in enhancing student employability.

Objectives
The key objectives of the case study were to:
1 Enhance student employability through work-based assessment for students undertaking Foundation degrees in hospitality.
2 Pilot different approaches for encouraging employer contribution to assessment design.
3 Investigate the relevance of the Foundation degree programme from the perspective of different employability stakeholders (student/employer/institution).
4 Generate findings to inform future developments across other programmes both within Westminster Kingsway College and beyond.

Context/rationale

Foundation degrees were developed and encouraged by the UK government, in part, to address the problem of skills shortages. Work-based learning and assessment are at the heart of the Foundation degree (FdA) philosophy at Westminster Kingsway College. The Hospitality Management FdA Course aims address the development of students so that they may progress 'within a range of careers in hospitality with an informed employment perspective' (Westminster Kingsway College 2007). The course aims also refer to the employability skills that students can expect to have acquired upon graduation. These include professional competence, self-reliance, interpersonal skills and critical practice, among others.

Higher education (HE) courses are expected to equip graduates to become immediate contributors in the workplace and yet it appears that employers are often still unsatisfied with the competencies of some of their new recruits. A particular change within the HE sector in the past decade or so is a more explicit approach to developing transferable employability skills within courses. Schuller (1995) refers to changes in the philosophical conception of a university. Over the past decade higher education has been described in terms of its role in economic competition. It must 'produce new graduates who will lead ... industry to victory in the worldwide technological competition' (Spring quoted in Hart, 1992 cited in Toohey, 1999).

University education today is seen by governments as a product whose sale may improve the balance of payments. Yorke and Knight (2004) talk about the 'politicisation of educational development' and argue that 'higher education is being driven by governmental expectations'. These expectations refer to the government's target of 50% of the population entering higher education by 2020 and leaving with employability skills. Yorke and Knight (2004) suggest that the promotion of 'skills' has met with limited acceptance by the higher education sector which has seen them as being 'narrowly-conceived, somewhat arbitrary and distinctly reductionist'.

Research by the Institute for Employment Studies (Hillage and Pollard, 1998) talks about employability skills in terms of 'baseline assets' (for example essential personal attributes such as reliability); 'intermediate assets' (for example generic occupational skills such as problem-solving); and 'high level assets' (for example, commercial awareness).

A view of the present and future nature of work is offered by Thompson and Warhurst (1998). They suggest that we are now living in a knowledge-based economy which is characterised by intense global competition. The trend will be away from routine work towards more creative, information, and people-focused activities; work will be about problem identification and problem-solving with rewards given for individual performance rather than seniority. According to these authors, the workplace will provide opportunities for creative expression, enhanced personal growth and professional autonomy. To succeed within this work environment, they suggest participants will need to display 'creative entrepreneurialism'. This has obvious implications for developing students' employability during their time at university.

Toohey (1999) advises that 'rethinking past approaches to higher education will be necessary to meet the changing needs of students and contexts' and suggests that HE must aim at more than 'intellectual development'. Government opinion is that a more skilled workforce is required and that it is the role of HE to become an 'economic saviour' (Toohey, 1999). In the recent past, it was the concern of government that degree courses concentrated too much on academic knowledge and too little on practical skills and personal attributes. The formal inclusion in the curriculum of 'transferable skills' was one development to stem from this concern.

While there seems to be little disagreement between academics and employers on the need to develop transferable skills, (Harvey and Knight, 1996 in Toohey, 1999) there are different opinions about how this can be achieved. Academics believe that such skills are a natural and intrinsic part of education. Employers, however, favour a more explicit approach and many report the difficulty in finding good graduate workers (People Management, 2005). Employers' criticism is often focused on graduates' lack of interpersonal or 'softer' skills.

Guirdham (1995) argues that interpersonal skills are crucial to organisational functioning. Examples of such attributes include; persuading, communication, influencing and negotiating skills, self-management, relationship building, self-knowledge and emotional resilience. Other skills cited as very important are information gathering, planning, objective setting, analytical skills, motivational skills, understanding cultural difference, independent learning, and problem-solving. It could be argued that many of these skills are natural components of work-based learning.

Foundation degrees

Because of the vocational nature of Foundation degrees, it is often expected that employers will be involved with their planning and validation, and that this is indeed a crucial element for their success. As an extension of this approach it may therefore be appropriate to suppose that employer involvement in the design of course assessment will help develop the relationship further. However, this is not necessarily a straightforward process and recent research (Sheehan, 2004) has indicated that there are issues surrounding the nature and level of employer engagement in terms of commitment levels, available time and consistency of judgement.

Quality assurance issues and processes can also be problematic in this regard.

At Westminster Kingsway College the FdA programmes are structured in two ways. Firstly, the full-time route which, in our experience, is more likely to be adopted by the younger student with a traditional academic background. Secondly, the day-release route specifically constructed for mature students already working full-time in the industry, who wish to gain a qualification whilst working. Whichever the route chosen, students are almost all working to a greater or lesser extent and therefore already have workplace experiences to bring into the classroom. Students with work experience are all too aware of employer expectations, and the gap which occurs from time to time between theory and practice. In order that students understand the relevance of their studies, it is crucial that course design (and teaching, learning and assessments activities) and the student learning experience is as 'real' as possible. The case study authors believe that work-based learning and assessment, and employer involvement, helps this happen.

When this case study commenced in 2005, Westminster Kingsway College's HE team had been working towards the effective integration of work-based learning (WBL) and assessment (WBA) on the Hospitality Management FdA programme and there were already successful instances where employers contributed towards the design and assessment of student assignments. An example of this was a leading bank's involvement with a module called *Small & Medium Sized Enterprise*. The success of this, and other similar collaborations, led to the recognition that employer involvement could positively impact on the quality of the student learning experience.

Therefore a primary goal of this case study was to investigate how employer involvement in the design, delivery and assessment of students' assignments could be best facilitated and encouraged to maximise student learning and employability, whilst at the same time recognising (amongst other issues already cited earlier in this case study) the inherent constraints traditionally associated with hospitality sector working patterns and hours.

Description

The project was scheduled to take place over a two-year period from September 2005. The initial phase (Phase 1) took place from September 2005 to June 2006 and focused specifically on the development of a work-related assessment (WRA) within the Hospitality Management FdA course. Phase 2 took place between September 2006 and June 2007 and involved the 'rolling out' of similar assessment approaches to other modules across different hospitality programmes offered at the College. It is worth pointing out that prior to the introduction of these particular assessments, the students had already been introduced to the concept of employ-ability skills through a *Personal Development* module involving workshops in which transferable skills are discussed. Students as part of that module were required to complete a personal skills audit and construct a personal development plan. This awareness and understanding of transferable/employability skills was used as a base from which to evaluate the intervention (i.e. students would be asked to feedback on how the assessment had contributed to their employability and which specific transferable skills they had developed).

The two phases of the case study project are detailed in the next section.

Phase one

❏ The FdA course team identified the specific module for development. Initially the *Conference and Event* module was selected for development as this practical area is regarded by many employers as very important to students' professional development for any future career in the hospitality industry.

❏ In addition many of the current and expected FdA hospitality students already have jobs within food & beverage and thus a work-based learning assignment in this area would be facilitated more readily. However, as it transpired the *Human Resource Management* (HRM) and *Principles of Management* (POM) modules were also subsequently selected for development (Appendix 1).

❏ In all three modules the existing assessment packages were reviewed using exter-nal employer feedback.

❏ The assessment programmes were redrafted in close consultation with one employer organisation (Mitchells & Butler) and more work-related assessment (WRA) elements were introduced so that specific aspects of the Yorke and Knight's 39 employability attributes could be developed and assessed (Yorke and Knight, 2006).

❏ The assessment vehicle consisted of a problem-based case study where the com-pany was seeking solutions from the students to real work-based problems; in this case the issues of management satisfaction, management development and progression in the leisure and entertainment sector.

❏ The assessment programmes were piloted with a specific group of FdA Hospitality students – 10 Level 5 day-release students. They were supported by collabora-tive delivery by one specific hospitality organisation, which offered classroom delivery and regular tutorial support as part of the support programme. On-line access to the company intranet was also made available to students.

❏ Three academic staff members were involved in the writing of the assessment and the co-ordination between classroom, students and employer.

❏ Mitchells & Butler's (M&B) Operations Resourcing Manager was involved with case study design and initial presentation to the students. Unit Managers from M&B were accessible to the students.

Phase two

❏ As a result of the relative success of Phase 1 it was intended to 'roll out' a similar problem-based WRA across other Foundation degree modules during academic year 2006-7.

❏ The team proposed to modify the scope and scale of these assessments, and in some cases to reduce levels of student workload whilst retaining the quality of the associated 'real life' experience. In other cases the potential to integrate further modules was examined so that substantial employer 'briefs' can be incorporated where it is deemed appropriate. It is also entirely appropriate that different subjects are considered together.

❏ It was intended to involve final-year undergraduate BA hospitality/tourism and business management students in this form of assessment, particularly where the employer briefs are more extensive or complex.

❏ Mitchells & Butler (M&B) were once more involved, and various options were discussed for possible assessment vehicles. One idea discussed was the development of an integrated assessment across modules (the team developed an assessment package for the final-year degree, Level 6, students studying a *Business Strategy* module and a *Marketing* module). However, after discussions with the employer, it was deemed more appropriate to design a more practical assessment for level 4 students.

❏ The *Food and Beverage* module was selected for the second intervention and the assessment required the students to work in groups on menu development and menu engineering at one of the Mitchells & Butler 'Castle Pub' outlets. The assessment used the students' knowledge of marketing theory which they had acquired during the previous semester study (Appendix 2).

Evaluation

It was recognised that the small number of students involved in Phase 1 of the research would make it more difficult to generalise from the findings. However this was primarily a single-case approach and it was felt by the course team that there were distinct benefits associated with working with a small group of students at this point, including an improved ability to track, monitor and gather rich observational data.

The module tutors and Mitchells & Butler managers jointly designed the assessment briefs. Academic staff and employer feedback on this development process indicated that the investment made by both parties in planning a WRL assignment resulted in a robust and industry-relevant assessment brief. The assessments both met the requirement of the organisation for solutions to real work problems and the students' need to meet the learning outcomes for specific modules.

Student feedback before, during and after the intervention indicates the positive benefits to be derived as a result of employer engagement in the delivery of some of the teaching sessions, and their ongoing support during the assessment process. Employer-led briefing workshops worked very well, as did a number of other activities including; escorted and unescorted workplace visits, ongoing on-line support and access to the company intranet within which some on-line dialogue took place between students and junior managers.

In terms of quality assurance processes required by the college, the newly designed assessments underwent the normal validation process and were subject to the college internal quality procedure of 'assessment review', where an independent academic colleague cross-checks the assignment brief against the learning outcomes for the module/course. The module assessments contained both individual and group elements. The assignment brief was also cross-checked for coherence, relevance and 'student appeal' by a senior member of M&B's HRM department.

The grades for students' WRL assignments were agreed in a decision-making process involving two key M&B senior managers and the module teams at Westminster Kingsway College. A simple employer observation/feedback set of documentation was developed which ensured that the employer views of performance fed into the students' overall result on a weighted basis. All members of the assessment team subsequently met to review results and discuss discrepancies. A 30% sample of assessment decisions underwent the normal 'assessment review stage 3' verification process as a further check on validity, reliability and consistency.

Student feedback on the process of undergoing this form of assessment was generally positive. There were some criticisms about the level of workload involved and the time factor associated with travel to various company sites and interviewing. This was particularly an issue with the students studying on a day-release basis. However there was a general consensus that there were substantial benefits from 'learning by doing' and undergoing assessment within a dynamic and stimulating environment which involved work-related learning.

Evidence suggests that students placed a much higher value on the process skills such as problem solving, having experienced this form of assessment. It was also evident from the first intervention that, despite the level of employer support provided, some students felt unduly anxious and 'stretched' by this form of assessment.

A comparison of results in these modules between the current and previous academic years does not show a significant change in the level of student performance although, in relation to Phase 1, it would appear that weaker students performed marginally more poorly.

Benefits to end users

Perceived benefits	
For students...	**For staff...**
Exposure to the workplace	Working with employers reinforces currency and relevance of course content
Employer involvement	
A realistic problem solving task	Ability to reinforce validity of employability skills
Commercial awareness	
Synthesis of theory and practice	Opportunity to avoid 'compartmentalising' of modules and encourages students to see the link between different subjects
Decision making	
Learning to work in groups	
Ability to integrate various subject areas	
Improved confidence	
Issues/Challenges	
For students...	**For staff...**
Some of the challenges often reported by students when undertaking group work were evident in this assignment.	Co-ordination of the process – need to ensure that all student groups get an equal experience
Group work presents a particular challenge for day-release students as they potentially struggle to find mutually convenient times to meet with fellow students.	Design of assessment is determined by employers' business needs – need to ensure all parties are satisfied

Discussion
Enablers that helped practice to work

❏ Previous collaboration with Barclays Bank which showed the mutual benefits of employer involvement.
❏ Positive relationship with Mitchells & Butler who were prepared to collaborate closely with the assessment design and management.
❏ Lecturers who were prepared to spend time developing assessments and amend teaching plans to facilitate the work-based assessment.
❏ Students who were responsive to the assessment.

Points of advice

Of the two interventions, Phase 2 was more successful in terms of the student learning experience and is a model we would like to use in the future. From our experience, when planning this type of assessment, consideration should be given to the stage in the course that employer involvement is used. The *Food and Beverage* module is taught during the first part of the course and appeared to help engage the students with the industry at an early stage. This sort of engagement with employers and the workplace affirms the relevance of the learning for students.

A benefit which derived from Phase 1 was the ability to integrate assessment across two modules. This helps students to become aware that, although most subjects are taught as stand alone modules, the various topics of a business programme are in fact strongly linked. Examples of combined assignment/assessments developed were in *Principles of Management* and *Human Resource Management* modules in Phase 1, and the *Food and Beverage* and *Marketing* modules in Phase 2.

Possible improvements/enhancers

To ensure the effectiveness of this approach to work-related learning, it is important that all students have the same opportunities to succeed. Evaluation during Phase 2 of the case study, revealed that the various groups of students had different experiences of the assessment. Obviously group dynamics always play an important part in the success or otherwise of group work – there will always be proactive students and less productive students. Similarly, there were pub managers who were willing to help the students and those who were not as generous with their time or information. It was evident from student feedback that the level of employer support and help differed between pubs and this affected students perceptions of the help/advice they had access to.

It is important therefore that the designers of a work-based assessment eliminate, as far as is possible, any variance of student experience and provide a level starting point from which to progress their investigation. This would be helped by more preparatory collaboration between lecturer, employer and business managers who are to be involved. One idea which came out of the feedback was to involve all the managers from the beginning, to gain their commitment, rather than after the assessment had been agreed by the employer and lecturer. Another potential benefit of this approach is that managers are often in the best position to suggest realistic work-based problems as the basis for the assignment, and would also be able to feedback to students at a sufficiently early stage in the students' research process.

External/internal commentary

Endorsement from the students, lecturers and employer confirm the efficacy of work-related assessment.

Students commented:

[The assessment] reinforced learning from other modules like research methods and marketing.

[The pub managers] were easily accessible.

It was really interesting speaking to people in industry.

The **lecturers** who were involved perceived work-related learning as a valuable tool and have said that they will continue to look for further opportunities to engage directly with a wider variety of employers to collaborate on opportunities for learning and assessment.

The *Food and Beverage* module leader believed that by completing the assessment based on actual pubs, the direct communication with the managers and site visits (as opposed to completing the assignment as a theoretical, classroom task) helped the students' understanding of the principles of product development significantly.

From the **employer's** point of view it appears that, in return for the investment of their time, they gain access to potential graduate recruits. It is also an opportunity to gain a fresh perspective on some of their organisational challenges – free consultancy as it were!

Conclusion
The development of an enhanced understanding of employability

Whilst it is true that the majority of the Foundation degree students are working while they are studying, it is evident that they often have limited appreciation of the concept of employability. They are often practitioners of employability without realising it. It is only when they are required to spend time in workshops analysing and reflecting on the skills and attributes which constitute employability that they begin to develop an awareness of how they can make a successful contribution to the workplace.

Certain aspects of employability have been specifically highlighted by the work-based assessment, such as the need for flexibility and the ability to solve problems. What has also become apparent to the students is the need for business awareness and that managers are usually working in a constantly changing external environment within the constraints of the organisation's internal pressures. This is an aspect of employability which becomes more obvious when the students are engaged in an investigative and/or problem solving task, and therefore ideally addressed by work-based assessment.

Further comments

The incorporation of work-based learning and work-based assessment is essential if we are to fulfil the objectives of our Foundation degree courses. Similarly, any institution delivering vocational courses needs to ensure that their courses reflect the industry their students are studying. By providing a programme which is relevant and current we are equipping students to take up positions of responsibility when they graduate. Part of this preparedness comes from bringing industry into the classroom and the experience of the two phases has reinforced the benefits of employer involvement and the need to develop and extend industrial relationships.

At the same time the research has indicated the limitations of employer contribution – what they are prepared to do and what they are not keen to do. This knowledge will be of significant benefit to the team when considering future vehicles for learning and assessment. Indeed it has already been of great value as the college has recently validated a Foundation degree course for Travelodge and this is a result of close collaboration between the institution and the organisation. The challenge now will be to deliver a course which addresses the needs of Travelodge as well as provide them with a valid industry wide vocational course.

References

Guirdham, M. (1995) *Interpersonal Skills at* Work. 2nd ed. London: Prentice Hall

Hillage, J. and Pollard, E. (1998) *Employability: Developing a framework for policy analysis.* Institute for Employment Studies

Jenkins, A., Breen, R. and Lindsay, R. (2003) *Reshaping Teaching in Higher Education.* London: Kogan Page

Knight, P. T. and Yorke, M. (2004) *Learning, Curriculum and Employability in higher education.* London: Routledge Falmer

People Management (2005) *Skills gap fuelled by graduate glut* **11** (23) 24th November p 13

Schuller, T. (1995) *The Changing University.* Buckingham: SRHE and Open University Press

Sheehan, C. (2004) Foundation Degree Assessment Models – Meeting the needs of 'new generation' students. Paper presented at the Council for Hospitality Management Education Conference, University of Wales Institute Cardiff, Cardiff, April

Toohey, S. (1999) *Designing Courses for Higher Education.* Buckingham: SRHE and Open University Press

Thompson, P. and Warhurst, C. (1998) Hands, Hearts and Minds: Changing Work and Workers at the end of the Century. In P. Thomson and C. Warhurst Eds *Workplaces of the Future.* Basingstoke: Macmillan

Westminster Kingsway College (2007) *Foundation Degree Hospitality Management Course Handbook 2007/08*

Yorke, M. and Knight, P. (2004) Being Strategic about employability *Journal of Educational Developments* **5** (4)

Yorke, M. and Knight, P. T. (2006) *Embedding employability into the curriculum.* Learning and Employability Series One. York: HEA Enhancing Student Employability Co-ordination Team p 8

Appendix 1   Assignment brief for *Human Resource Management and Principles of Management* module

ASSESSMENT RECORD FORM	
Student Name:	
Module:	Human Resource Management & Principles of Management
Module value:	60 credits total
Lecturer:	Vivien Mutucumarana & Linda Waghorn
Assessment no.	Collaborative Assessment Project with Mitchells & Butler Ltd. Consultant - Mr A Knight HRM
Assessment method:	Individual summary followed by a group report & individual essay. Seminar to form the basis of a presentation to the board of Mitchells & Butler.
Assessment weighting:	100%
Date of Submission:	On time ❑ Late ❑
Length:	
Learning Outcomes Assessed. Skills Mapped	**HRM** Explore the issues of Human Resource Planning Understand HRM processes e.g. discipline, training and counselling and grievance. Consider legislative principles of employment contracts. **Management** Differentiate between key function of management Evaluate various management approaches and styles. Critically analyse the theories of leadership approaches Apply the principles of group development Evaluate communication and decision making process Diagnose organisation cultures and structures and appreciate their impact on management of change. Managing information; communication

Brief

You are asked to assume the role of research assistant, and contribute to a group project aimed at improving the workplace performance at Mitchells & Butler. Working in groups, you will use a range of research methods to provide ideas of effective human resource management. Your work will demonstrate understanding of management theory applied to operational or human resource management.

Work to Produce

Task 1   Individual summary of key issues

You are asked to attend the Mitchells & Butler briefing session with Mr A Knight in week two. Submit a summary of the key issues to your tutor in class in week three.

Weighting 10%, word count 250–500.

Task 2   Group Work to produce an outline of research to be undertaken

Group document

Attend a group meeting to agree a summary of the key issues to be addressed, & propose a specific issue or area of work for your research project. The proposed topic should be signed by your tutor & colleagues and submitted in your group report. It must indicate how the group is to organise research undertaken, indicating the work of each individual for task 3.   Weighting 10%, word count 250.

Task 3   Group Report

Produce a group report on the topic agreed with your tutor. You may wish to select from the list below, or compile your own proposal.

1   Investigate the performance of either management trainees or management grades, identifying links with the leadership qualities of individuals.

2   Examine recruitment strategies at Mitchells and Butler, commenting on the impact on retention & motivation of staff.

3   Analyse reward structures in place at Mitchells and Butler, & the impact on performance. Comment on the links between rewards structures, management structure and culture in place at this organisation.

4   Examine management within the organisation structure at Hollywood Bowl Retail, & comment on the impacts on retention and progression of managers.

Weighting 30%, word count 3,000–3,500.

Note

Group Work assessment will be ongoing, notes may be taken by tutors that contribute to the group work mark. A 10-mark reduction or increase may be awarded to individuals based on knowledge of topics & group contribution.

Task 4 (a)   Individual Essay, HRM

In class time, and based on your experience in carrying out tasks 1–3, provide an individual essay which reflects on group behaviour and related ethical issues in the workplace.   Weighting 30%, word count 500.

Task 4 (b)   Individual Essay – Principles of management

Task 5   Presentations to select students to address the Board of Mitchells & Butler

Present your findings to the Board of Directors on the research undertaken in task 3.

Weighting 20%

Appendix 2   Assignment brief for *Food and Beverage* module

ASSESSMENT RECORD FORM			
Student Name:			
Module:	FOOD AND BEVERAGE.		
Module value:	15 CREDITS at LEVEL 4		
Lecturer:	DAVID THOMSON.		
Assessment no.	Assessment 1 (Full-time Students)		
Assessment method:	Report & Short Presentation		
Assessment weighting:	50%		
Date of Submission:		On time ❑	Late ❑
Length:	1,500		
Learning Outcomes Assessed.	1 Evaluate the operational and economic characteristics of food and beverage operations.		
	2 Evaluate the product and service development of food and beverage operations.		
Skills mapped:	Managing information.		
	Communication skills.		
	Professional working practices.		

Brief

You will be required to attend a presentation by Mitchells & Butler at one of the Castle Pubs in London at the beginning of March in order to receive further details of the task. Please await further instruction from your tutor

Following the presentation by Mitchells & Butler you will then be required to produce an *individual 1,500-word report* and a *group (3–4 people) 15-minute presentation*.

Task 1   Presentation

The presentation will require the group of students to present their research, findings, recommendations and implementation plan to a panel.

The panel will consist of the module tutor, representative from Mitchells & Butler, media services (recording the presentations) and, at times, a further to tutor to moderate the presentations.

Task 2   Report

Students will also be required to submit an individual 1,500-word report that provides their individual understanding of the research, findings, recommendations and implementation plan.

You will be required to underpin this understanding with the relevant theory, analysis and evaluation of food and beverage operations. This should include the following information:

❑ 'background history' to the outlet's environment
❑ the nature of food and beverage products on offer in the outlet
❑ patterns of demand and scope of business
❑ customer profile
❑ the average spending power.

9

Personal Development Planning in the delivery and assessment of graduate employability skills

Bob Snape *University of Bolton*

This case study explores the use of Personal Development Planning as a means of assessing students awareness of, and confidence in, a range of employability skills

The aim of this case study was to enhance students' awareness of graduate employability skills through the use of personal development planning (PDP). To achieve this, a first-year module combining study skills and PDP was developed as the basis of an intervention. At the start of the module students were asked to undertake a self-evaluation of their competency across a range of generic skills.

University Careers Service staff and employers were involved in the delivery of the module, skills development and assessment. At the end of the module students completed a second self-evaluation of their generic skills and also participated in focus-group interviews designed to elicit their view of the module and the extent to which it had encouraged them to integrate employability skills within their personal development planning. It was found that when generic and transferable skills were delivered as 'employability skills', students were less engaged than when, in a repeat of the intervention, they were presented as 'career development skills'.

The intervention was successful in encouraging students to create personal development plans which incorporated longer term career planning. The engagement of specialist career development staff in the delivery of the intervention was a positive step which enhanced the breadth of the intervention and is recommended to other educators as good practice. The case study suggests that as students tended to prefer practical and experiential learning methods, curriculum-integrated approaches to the delivery of career development skills should be considered.

Objectives

The overall aim of the study was to explore ways in which students could be engaged in personal development planning as a way of developing their awareness of employability, career development and the importance of generic, as distinct from subject, skills. The three principal objectives were:

1   To identify ways in which PDP offers opportunities for the delivery and /or assessment of employability skills.
2   To evaluate the perceived relevance of PDP to employment amongst students and employers.
3   To identify ways of strengthening the contribution of PDP to students' employability.

Context/rationale

The University of Bolton has traditionally exhibited a strong commitment to the provision of work-related higher education and this is reflected in the vocational orientation of courses provided by the School of Health and Social Sciences. The University has a firm commitment to widening participation which is reflected in the profile of students within the School and the fact that the majority of sport management and tourism students enter with vocational rather than academic qualifications. It was recognised that the students involved in the intervention were, in terms of previous educational experience, vocationally/career orientated and could be expected to have an interest in their own employability. Furthermore, it was anticipated that they would need support in enhancing their study skills to cope with the first year of university, particularly the relative degree of independence in learning and the predominance of written forms of assessment, including examinations.

In support of the strategic direction outlined above, the university has in recent years introduced a number of learning and teaching initiatives to ensure that students are able to make an effective transition from further to higher education and that they develop not only subject specific, but generic skills. Examples of such initiatives are the inclusion of assessed work placements and, in the light of the Dearing Report (NCIHE, 1997), the development of learning outcomes based on key and generic skills (see also Becket and Kemp, 2006). More recently, the school has offered a first-year generic skills module to students undertaking leisure, sport and tourism management courses that teaches study skills and introduces students to some of the generic employability skills such as team working, self-management and an ability to be responsible for their own learning referred to by Dearing. In September 2005 the University adopted a standard framework of Personal Development Planning (PDP) to enable students to have access to a range of learning opportunities intended to support the development and assessment of their employability skills. In doing so the university was helping establish an existing trend in which the delivery of employability skills has been linked to widening participation and PDP (Thomas and Jones, 2007; Ward, 2006).

The project thus offered an opportunity to not only support the school in the introduction and development of PDP in its curriculum but to explore the extent to which students could be encouraged to view PDP as a useful tool in obtaining employment. It also created an opportunity for teaching staff to learn about the ways in which students can, from the beginning of their three-year university career, be supported in developing an awareness of the importance of generic skills whilst at the same time developing their subject knowledge and job-specific practical skills. The project also offered a learning opportunity for staff to develop their understanding of the design and delivery of a curriculum capable of developing employability skills (Yorke and Knight, 2006). The module that formed the basis of the intervention was delivered to a combined group of sport development, tourism management and international tourism management students. The intervention module was delivered twice to different intakes of first-year students. The first occurrence (autumn 2005) involved approximately 50 students, the second (autumn 2006) approximately 30 students. Both cohorts consisted mainly of students from the United Kingdom, predominantly the Greater Manchester region, but also included a number of tourism students from mainland Europe.

Description

The intervention was based on the delivery of a first-year first-semester module, *Business Skills and Personal Development*. The aim of this module was to develop students' study and learning skills to enable them to adapt to their first year in higher education and also to develop their awareness of, and competency in, a range of generic skills such as time management, team working, problem-solving and personal development planning. The module offered an opportunity to encourage students to nurture an awareness of the long-term importance of generic skills for their career and to integrate the development of these skills within their personal development planning process. The module was delivered in fourteen three-hour slots by a leisure-management subject lecturer. It was felt that the generic nature of the module and the mixed-subject background of the student cohort obviated the need for the allocation of a subject specialist to each sub-group of the cohort.

The assessment framework of the module required students to undertake two assignments; a small group-based presentation on a specific generic skill and, second, the production of a personal development plan at the end of the module. The delivery of the module was constructed around the understanding and development of specific skills. The subject content and delivery schedule of the module were as follows:

Table 1 *Business Skills and Personal Development* module

Week	Topic
1	Introduction to Module. Becoming an Undergraduate. Self-Evaluation of Skills. Time Management & Study Schedules
2	Personal development planning. Note-taking in Lectures and Seminars
3	Finding, evaluating and using information; Library Skills Group Presentation Preparation
4	Writing Essays and Reports. Citation.
5	Planning and Delivering Presentations
6	Team working
7	Individual Tutorials
8	Individual Tutorials
9	Group Presentations
10	Revising for Examinations & Examination Techniques
11	PDP Workshop
12	Review of Presentations / PDP/ Report Final Workshop
13	Tutorials
14	Module Review

First Phase   Autumn 2005

The first delivery of the module involved approximately 50 students drawn from sport development and tourism management courses. Lectures outlining the individual skills were delivered at the start of each session. The remainder of the three-hour teaching session was given over to practical work in which the students were placed in small groups to prepare their first assignment (i.e. group preparation for and delivery of a presentation on a specific skill). This was intended to develop their awareness of the importance of skills such as teamwork, leadership, problem-solving, information retrieval and oral communication.

Students were informed during the first teaching session that they were participants in a national project on the enhancement of employability skills. They were asked to complete pre- and post-intervention questionnaire (see Appendix 1).

The pre-intervention questionnaire, which was distributed at the commencement of the first session, sought to identify students' perceptions of their own confidence and ability in a range of interpersonal and study skills related to employability (e.g. team working, adaptability, self-confidence, writing skills, ability to reflect on their own performance and sensitivity to the needs of others).

At the end of the module the students were asked to re-evaluate their perceived competence in these same skills and to use this information to prepare their personal development plan and action plan. Only 5.3% of the students had a personal development plan at the start of the module, though 18.4% claimed to have a written action plan. On completion of the module 54.8% had both a personal development plan and an action plan. The intervention can thus be seen to have affected an increase in the number of students actively engaged in personal development planning, though the percentage of positive responses was surprisingly low given the fact that the production of a PDP was a principal element of the assessment strategy of the module. This suggests that the intervention was not highly successful in engaging students' commitment to using personal development planning as a means of enhancing their employability at this stage of their university career.

The responses to the pre- and post-intervention questionnaires produced some surprising results. Overall the students rated themselves highly in the pre-intervention questionnaires on the majority of the listed skills and attributes. Later experience of the module and coursework suggested that many had over-estimated the levels of their skills and attributes. This may have been partly attributable to the fact that approximately two thirds of the cohort currently held a part-time job and may have interpreted this as evidence of a number of the listed skills and attributes. Another possible factor may be that their judgment was based on performance and feedback in further education. A further possibility is that their assessment was based on youthful confidence and inexperience. This was noted by a mature student later in the intervention who commented that:

> I was aware of the skills required by an employer. As a mature student I do not feel that I was as confident as the younger students but my maturity has helped and supported me in other ways.

The responses to the post-intervention questionnaire suggest that, following their experience of the first semester at university, students felt less confident in their skills and attributes overall. Table 2 indicates changes in levels of confidence in specific skills and attributes; it is noteworthy that the responses indicate increased confidence in only four skills or attributes, namely a desire to learn, writing essays and reports, personal development planning and teamwork.

Table 2 Comparative responses of the pre- and post-intervention questionnaires

Skill / Attribute	Pre-intervention (n=38)		Post-intervention (n=24)	
	Not Confident	Confident	Not Confident	Confident
Self-awareness	18.4	81.6	29.8	70.9
Self-confidence	29.0	71.0	42.0	58.0
Ability to work independently	13.1	86.9	16.1	83.9
Sensitive to needs of others	21.1	78.9	32.2	67.8
Adaptable	10.5	89.5	19.3	80.7
Desire to learn	13.2	86.8	12.9	**87.1**
Reflect on own performance	23.7	76.3	32.2	67.8
Address a group	31.6	68.4	48.4	51.6
Effective reader	39.4	60.6	45.2	54.8
Finding information	31.5	68.5	45.2	54.8
Writing essays and reports	47.4	52.6	35.4	**64.6**
Listening	15.7	84.2	19.3	80.7
Personal Development Planning	52.6	47.4	48.4	**51.6**
Team working	15.8	84.2	6.5	**93.7**
Problem-solving	13.1	86.9	22.6	77.4
Using initiative	13.1	86.9	22.6	77.4

A degree of caution is necessary when comparing the results of the pre- and post-intervention questionnaires because of a difference in the number of respondents at each stage. Nevertheless, it is interesting to note that at the end of the module, with a small number of exceptions, students generally felt less confident in many generic skills; notably self-awareness, self-confidence, the ability to address a group and the ability to display sensitivity to the needs of others. This may reflect a degree of over-confidence in the responses to the pre-intervention questionnaire in that having been asked to demonstrate their abilities in one or more of the skills covered, students were able to express a more realistic, evidence-based and self-reflective assessment of their levels of competence.

Further, it was notable that those skills or attributes in which the students felt more confident tended to be those in which they had experienced some practical involvement during the semester. They had all produced a written course assignment, had worked as a team in the preparation of a group presentation and had been required to develop a personal development plan.

When asked in a further question which employability skills they had most improved upon during the period if the intervention, the skill most widely cited was teamwork (n19), followed by time management (n9), and delivering a presentation (n9). However, there were low numbers of citations of perceived improvement in some other skills. For example note-taking (n2), reading (n2), and report-writing (n2). This may reflect the fact that the students had not gained sufficient experience in these skills in between the pre- and post-questionnaires; it may also reflect the inherent subjectivity of the questions. A full list of the responses to this question is contained in Appendix 2.

Second Phase   Autumn 2006

The module was repeated in the academic year 2006–07. In the light of the limited number of responses to the post-intervention questionnaire in the previous year, a number of modifications were made to the intervention. The phrase 'employability skills' was abandoned in favour of 'professional and career skills' as feedback suggested that the former had appeared a vague and confusing term to some students in the first cohort. The notion of career was also felt to be more appropriate to students embarking upon a course that was expected to lead to employment.

The principal modification in this second phase of the project was the engagement of the university's careers service staff in the delivery and evaluation of the module. Student feedback on the first phase also indicated that they would have liked more opportunities to develop skills in a practical context. While the university does have a compulsory work-experience module, this is delivered only in the second year and it was felt important to find a way of involving an employer in the first year to give credence to the delivery of 'career' and 'professional' skills. The careers service staff approached an external trainer employed by a national car hire firm who delivered a number of sessions in which students participated in a range of games designed to develop their awareness of and competence in a range of generic skills; namely listening, team work, leadership and communication. The students clearly enjoyed this form of delivery and responded well to it.

The use of a post-intervention questionnaire to elicit feedback was not repeated; instead a number of focus groups, conducted by a member of the university careers service, were undertaken. It was felt that students would be more open and comfortable in expressing their views to a member of staff who was not also involved in the delivery and assessment of their course. Unfortunately attendance at the pre-arranged focus groups was disappointing and the range of responses was consequently limited. The responses that were received were generally favourable. Again it was felt that the module had been useful in raising awareness of, and development of, generic skills.

Evaluation

The intervention was in the main useful to students in raising their awareness of generic skills, not only in the context of their course but also in relation to their employability.

At the end of Phase One, the responses to the questions on skills development suggested an association between skills development and practical experience-based learning. The skills most heavily cited as instances of perceived improvement – teamwork, the delivery of a presentation and time management – were amongst those most readily practised in the module through the group-based presentation assignment and the requirement for the students to keep a time diary. This finding suggests that the concept of a generic-skills module is inherently fraught with challenge as it is difficult and occasionally impossible to create opportunities for the practice of a wide range of employability skills within the first fourteen weeks of a student's university career. Familiarity with the principles of a skill is clearly not the same as competence in it. Nevertheless, the majority of the students felt that the module had enabled them to acquire a better understanding of employability skills. Examples of comments from students were:

I feel more confident applying for a job now.

I am aware of many more skills and think this will be a great help in the future.

I now know what I need to develop and improve upon.

Aligned to this was an overall view that the module had been useful, not only in enabling them to become more aware of the existence of employability skills, but in encouraging them to be aware of the desirability of enhancing their competence in them.

It made me look at the skills I need in my career.

It was the only time that I have ever looked at specific skills.

Interestingly one student also thought about this in terms of *being* an employer:

It helped me to understand what skills and targets I would need to achieve in order
to get myself into a good job or to be a good employer.

Students were asked to comment on ways they felt the module might be improved. Some disquiet had been expressed, particularly by some sport development students, about being in a vocationally mixed group with tourism students. Although it was explained that the generic content of the module transcended subject field boundaries, some residual dissatisfaction remained on this account, as evidenced in the comment that 'it could have been more relevant to the course'.

Finally, students were asked to say how they intended to develop their employability skills after the module. This was an important question as it related to the aim of the intervention in terms of encouraging students to develop personal development and action plans. Six students referred specifically to an intention to use action planning and their comments reflect an understanding of the long-term benefits of personal development planning:

> I intend to continue to learn and maintain the flow of work though my PDP and action plan.
>
> I intend to keep practising the skills in each of my other modules.
>
> I have to continue to develop these skills as it has been a long time since essays and referencing. Also, as a mature student, I feel I have to work twice as hard to justify being at university.

At the close of Phase Two it became clear that the practical sessions provided by the external employer were particularly well-received. Students were able to cite leadership, teamwork, honesty, reliability, management, communication and independent working as skills and attributes employers were likely to be interested in. The second phase also suggested that the teaching of generic skills through games and 'fun' activities is a specialist skill and requires deep knowledge not just of theoretical content but also of a range of appropriate activities. This is particularly true of those generic skills which are not as easily identified as study skills, for example leadership, teamwork, negotiation and adaptability. The delivery of modules with similar objectives to that under review here is not infrequently allocated to subject staff who may not always be adequately equipped to offer the most effective delivery. The involvement of specialist careers staff in the second occurrence enhanced the range of delivery and introduced specialist expertise that would not have otherwise been available.

The results point to a number of conclusions. Students in both phases preferred to learn generic skills through practical exercises. In some cases these arose naturally through the delivery of the curriculum, as for example in planning and delivering presentations or in writing reports. Other skills, however, did not have as overt a curriculum presence and it was more difficult to deliver these in a practical sense, certainly for a subject lecturer who did not have a background or training in this area. In contrast, the engagement of an external person who was not from an employment background in leisure, sport or tourism but who *did* have expertise in generic skills training through practical games-based activities was highly successful.

Discussion
Enablers that helped practice to work

1   The involvement of staff members of the university's Careers Services was crucial to the success of the intervention. Although they were involved only in the second phase of the project, their expertise in careers education and their ability – through their professional networks – to engage external-employer involvement in the delivery of the intervention, introduced a step-change in the nature of the intervention. Careers staff conducted a number of focus groups with the students which ensured a greater degree of objectivity than would have been possible with a member of the lecturing staff.

2   The support of members of the project staff in the input of questionnaire data in SSPS was a further important form of enabling support.

3   The engagement of a trainer employed by an external organisation in the second phase of the intervention was significant in enhancing the quality of the intervention.

Points of advice

1   When the intervention was first introduced to the students the term 'employability' was to match its use in the project title. However, the students' concept of employability was influenced by the fact that most of them were employed, usually in part-time work, though some had previously been in full-time employment. On this basis they felt, understandably, that they possessed the skills necessary to employment. This presented challenges in encouraging them to think in terms of the employability skills deficit that was assumed by the project. In the second year the phrase 'career development skills' was used in preference and this appeared to have a greater appeal to the students. This finding corresponds with other research (Alpern, 1997) on the delivery of employability skills which suggests that not only students, but staff too, may find the term confusing.

2   It was found that the initial questionnaire (Appendix 1) did not yield the expected data as the majority of students did not respond fully to the open questions, even though class time was allocated to the task. The introduction of focus groups in the second year provided a more effective method of exploring the relevant issues.

Possible improvements/enhancers

Given the students' positive reactions to the practical sessions delivered by the external industrial trainer, the intervention could be improved by the utilisation of a

Benefits to end-users

Perceived benefits

For students...	For staff...
Raised awareness of the importance of generic skills to their employability and career development	Enhancement of students' abilities to manage their transition into higher education
Opportunities for self-evaluation of competence in a range of generic skills	Enhancement of the vocational orientation of the curriculum
Introduction to personal development planning and action planning	Opportunity to work with specialist Careers Service staff in the university by engaging them in the delivery of the intervention
Production of a personal development plan	
Opportunities to develop practical employability skills	
The use of personal development plans to improve employability skills	

Issues/Challenges

For students...	For staff...
The initial self-evaluation of skills revealed that students often believed they possessed a higher level of ability than proved to be the case. This may have led them to feel that the intervention was superfluous to their needs and although later experience would have suggested this was not the case, they could not have known this in an objective sense until a later stage of the first academic year	Maintaining a balance between the academic and the skills elements of the course
Continuity of focus on employability beyond the intervention was not assured	Engaging and enthusing students in the development of generic skills and dealing with the dislike expressed by some students of a module devoted to generic as opposed to subject skills
Many students found some difficulty in accepting that the intervention was worthwhile. Some felt that it was inappropriate because it was not subject specific and disliked being in a mixed subject group. For example, in dealing with referencing, examples were given of both sport and tourism text citations. Some students failed to understand that examples from both subject areas were relevant to them	The wide range of skills addressed
The wide range of skills addressed, some of which were not adequately supported by available learning resources	The timing of the intervention ought to be reviewed

problem-solving and task orientated approach. In furtherance of this observation, some recent research (Cranmer, 2006) has suggested that employer involvement in course delivery and employment based training may be more effective than delivery by academic subject experts. A further consideration may be that a too wide range of skills was addressed. Some interventions in this field have addressed a narrower range (Holmes and Miller, 2000) and in view of the relatively short duration of the intervention under review, the adopted range was possibly too ambitious.

External/internal commentary
Two comments from the principal stakeholders – the students who *undertook the intervention* module – may serve as testimony to the value of the project to them:

> Very encouraging; it has made me address my strengths and weaknesses, which I was not generally aware of.
>
> There are more employability skills that I need to think about. Some, I didn't really think they mattered.

Conclusion
This case study suggests, among other things, that while the term 'employability' may be useful in describing an overall 'fitness for employment', it is difficult to relate this to the curriculum. In the author's opinion, greater distinction needs to be made between skills that can be taught – for example writing, presenting and time management – and attributes that cannot be taught; for example, self-awareness, reliability and a desire to learn. Despite the current political pressures on higher education providers to produce employable graduates (not in itself an unworthy objective) it may be unwise to promise to deliver what cannot always be produced.

It is possible however to help students to acquire the skills that might be expected of a graduate in a professional employment sector, especially where these can equate to professional qualifications. The students found the concept of 'professional' and 'career development' skills more easily understandable than 'employability' skills. The reason for this appears to relate to the need to imply some distinction between the level of skills expected of them as graduates, and the skills level they believed they currently possessed through their part-time employment in largely unskilled part-time jobs.

References
Alpern, M. (1997) Critical workplace competencies: essential? Generic? Core? Employability? Non-technical? What's in a name? *Canadian Vocational Journal* **32** (4) pp. 6–16

Becket, N. and Kemp, P. Eds. (2006) *Enhancing Graduate Employability in Business and Management,*

Hospitality, Leisure, Sport and Tourism. Newbury: Threshold Press

Cranmer, S. (2006) Enhancing graduate employability: best intentions and mixed outcomes. *Studies in Higher Education* **31** (2) pp 169–184

Holmes, A. and Miller, S. (2000) A Case for Advanced Skills and Employability in Higher Education. *Journal of Vocational Education and Training* **52** (4) pp. 653–664

NCIHE (1997) National Committee of Enquiry into Higher Education (1997) *Higher Education in the Learning Society* Norwich: HMSO

Thomas, L and Jones, R. (2007) *Embedding employability in the context of widening participation.* Higher Education Academy, Learning and Employability Series 2

Ward, R. et al (2006) Personal *development planning and employability.* Higher Education Academy, Learning and Employability Series 2

Yorke, M. (2006) *Employability in higher education: what it is–what it is not.* Higher Education Academy, Learning and Employability Series 1

Yorke, M. and Knight, P. T. (2006) *Embedding employability into the curriculum.* Higher Education Academy, Learning and Employability Series 1

Appendix 1
The Phase One pre- and post-intervention questionnaires
Pre-intervention questionnaire Autumn 2005

1.   Course Details

1.1   What is the title of your course (in full)?

1.2   Are you studying full or part time?

1.3   If part time, what is your current job?

1.4   Please provide details of any part-time work you currently undertake (Nature of the work and number of hours per week)

2.   Your Degree and Your Career

2.1.1   What kind of job do you hope to secure on graduation? Please be as specific as possible, e.g. sport development officer, tourism sales manager, assistant leisure centre management, fitness adviser. Please enter 'Undecided' if you are not sure.

2.1.2   Do you have a written Personal Development Plan? (please tick box)
YES❑   NO❑

2.1.3   Do you have a written action plan to help you achieve your academic and career targets? (please tick box)   YES❑ NO❑

2.2   How important to your future career do you think the following aspects of your degree course will be? (please tick relevant column)

1=not important 3=not sure 5=very important

	1	2	3	4	5
2.2.1 Subject Knowledge					
2.2.2 People Management Skills					
2.2.3 Information Technology Skills					

2.2.4	Writing Skills					
2.2.5	Research Skills					
2.2.6	Personal Development Planning					
2.2.7	Work Experience					
2.2.8	Presentation Skills					
2.2.9	Work Experience					
2.2.10	Other (please specify)					

3   **Career Planning**
To what extent do you feel confident that you possess the following attributes and skills?
(please tick relevant column)

1=not at all confident 3=not sure 5=very confident

3.1	Self awareness					
3.2	Self confidence					
3.3	Ability to work independently					
3.4	Sensitive to needs of others					
3.5	Adaptable					
3.6	Desire to learn					
3.7	Ability to reflect on my own performance					
3.8	Ability to address a group					
3.9	Effective reading					
3.10	Finding information					
3.11	Writing essays and reports writer					
3.12	Listening					
3.13	Personal Development Planning					
3.14	Team working					
3.15	Problem Solving					
3.16	Using my own initiative					
3.17	Clear idea of the career I wish to follow					
3.18	Clear about which skills I need to develop					

4   Employability Skills in your degree course (i.e. general skills you think employers look for in candidates)
Please list five skills you would like to develop while at university that you believe will make you a more employable graduate:

1	
2	
3	
4	
5	

5   Personal Details

5.1	Gender	Male	
		Female	
5.2	Age	18 – 20	
		21 – 25	
		26 – 30	
		Over 30	

5.3   Nationality

5.4   How would you describe your ethnic status?

Thank you for completing this questionnaire. It is part of a national research project to help universities improve the development of students' employability potential.

Post-intervention questionnaire Spring 2006

1.   Course Details

1.1   What is the title of your course (in full)?

1.2   Are you studying full or part time?

1.3   If part time, what is your current job?

1.4   Please provide details of any part-time work you currently undertake
        (Nature of the work and number of hours per week)

2.2   **How important to your future career do you think the following aspects of your degree
        course will be? (please tick relevant column)**

        1=not important 3=not sure 5=very important

		1	2	3	4	5
2.2.1	Subject Knowledge					
2.2.2	People Management Skills					
2.2.3	Information Technology Skills					
2.2.4	Writing Skills					
2.2.5	Research Skills					
2.2.6	Personal Development Planning					
2.2.7	Work Experience					
2.2.8	Presentation Skills					
2.2.9	Work Experience					
2.2.10	Other (please specify)					

3   Graduate Attributes and Career Planning
     To what extent do you feel confident that you possess the following attributes and skills?
     (please tick relevant column)

                    1=not at all confident 3=not sure 5=very confident

		1	2	3	4	5
3.1	Self awareness					
3.2	Self confidence					
3.3	Ability to work independently					
3.4	Sensitive to needs of others					
3.5	Adaptable					
3.6	Desire to learn					
3.7	Ability to reflect on my own performance					
3.8	Ability to address a group					
3.9	Effective reading					
3.10	Finding information					
3.11	Writing essays and reports					
3.12	Listening					
3.13	Personal Development Planning					
3.14	Team working					
3.15	Problem Solving					
3.16	Using my own initiative					
3.17	Clear idea of the career I wish to follow					
3.18	Clear about which skills I need to develop					

4   Employability Skills in your degree course
     Please list five skills you feel you have developed in this module that you believe will make
     you a more employable graduate:

1
2
3
4
5

5   Developing Employability Skills

5.1   Do you feel you have a better understanding of employability skills now than you did
      before undertaking the module?

5.2   To what extent was this module useful in encouraging you to think about employability
      skills?

5.3   How could it have been improved?

5.4   How do you intend to develop your employability skills after the end of the module?

6   Personal Details

6.1   Gender

Male	
Female	

6.2   Age

18 – 20	
21 – 25	
26 – 30	
Over 30	

6.3   Nationality

6.4   How would you describe your ethnic status?

Thank you for completing this questionnaire. It is part of a national research project to help universities improve the development of students' employability potential.

Appendix 2   Perception of the five employability skills and attributes most developed in Phase One 2005–06

Number of citations	Skill
19	teamwork
9	delivery of a presentation, time management
8	increased self-confidence, listening to others
5	finding information, essay writing
4	desire to learn, adaptability, IT skills, writing skills, referencing
3	self awareness, organisation, communication skills
2	use of initiative, work independently, personal development planning, self-reflection, note taking, preparation, reading skills, problem solving
1	setting own targets, being reliable, report writing, negotiating, work experience, subject knowledge

10

Employability enhancement for new students approaching a work-experience year

Charles Whittaker *Oxford Brookes University*

This case study examines how students' employability skills are enhanced through preparation for work placement

This case study aims to evaluate the impact of incorporating employability skills into a first year undergraduate module designed, in part, to prepare students for work placement. The term 'employability' is used in its wider sense to encompass knowledge, analytical and learning skills as well as job-application/seeking skills. The project explored student perceptions of the importance of employability skills through a self-completion questionnaire administered with two cohorts of students at the beginning and end of a first year module *Understanding Hospitality Businesses*. There were 150 student participants in the first cohort and 130 in the second.

The results demonstrate that students rate 'subject knowledge' highly in terms of enhancing employability when they arrive at the university and after the module, but that a significant increase in awareness of the importance of job-hunting skills occurs through embedding activities such as analysing employer needs, CV preparation and interviewing skills. By embedding such skills into the structure of the module they are generally accepted as a valid part of student learning and may result in a more employable candidate in terms of knowledge, business skills and in job seeking capabilities.

Objectives

The case study objectives were:

1 To provide students with greater employability skills for their work-experience year (and later employment) both in terms of knowledge and transferable skills, particularly in job-seeking capabilities.
2 To measure the perceived change in students' knowledge and understanding

of the importance of employability skills at the start and end of a compulsory first-year module.

3   To identify future opportunities to improve the module in relation to enhancing students' employability.

4   To identify successful strategies that might be applicable in other modules or courses.

Context/rationale

Lees (2002: 6) provides a basic definition of employability as the 'ability to obtain initial employment'. However employability is about more than getting a job. Perhaps more useful is the definition offered by the Centre for Employability at the University of Central Lancashire (UCLan), which extends the definition to 'being successful in a chosen job for the benefit of all stakeholders'. UCLan also point to the importance that government places on the subject, particularly in relation to the role of higher education (HE) in developing these skills.

One difficulty in attempting to define employability is its multidimensional nature and the need to distinguish between the skills needed to be successful in a job, and those needed to obtain one. These 'job' skills are further broken down into knowledge about the work environment, and 'key' or generic skills such as communication, numeracy, information technology and learning how to learn (Dearing, 1997). Broader attributes such as personal attitudes and self-belief are also recognised as important. Lees (2002) further highlights the importance of lifelong learning, team working and reflective thinking, though it might be argued that these do not quite fit with Lees' rather narrow definition of obtaining initial employment.

The University and Department of Hospitality, Leisure and Tourism Management

Oxford Brookes University is a post-1992 'new' university. In 2006–07 it had 18,768 students enrolled on courses ranging from Foundation degrees to postgraduate courses. Undergraduates form 73% of the student population, and the largest percentage of students is studying business and administration courses (17.6% of the total enrolled students). The Department of Hospitality, Leisure and Tourism Management is part of the University Business School, and has been offering hospitality courses for more than 50 years. The Department has more than 900 students studying a range of undergraduate and postgraduate qualifications in hospitality and tourism.

Three of the five undergraduate courses require students to undertake a compulsory one-year paid work placement and this takes place in year 2 of a four-year sandwich degree. The preparation of students for work placement is a key focus in the first year of study. Various authors on employability mention the need to explain to students the importance of employability and to highlight where it is embedded in the curriculum and individual modules (Yorke and Knight, 2006). However, most studies seem to examine employability in terms of graduating students and thus have different emphases and focus than the one adopted for this case study. The needs of employability in relation to work placement, and to preparing first year students in this instance, are more focused on the transition from school to university and introducing students (often for the first time as a full-time employee) to the world of work.

At a curriculum level, the department is, by its nature, vocationally oriented and therefore it tends to be more aware of the need for employability development. This vocational orientation also, arguably, increases the importance of including employability as a key focus of core modules within the courses it operates. The undergraduate 'sandwich' courses typically run for four years and involve a one-year placement in the hospitality and tourism industries, and the first-year modules deal with both the transition to HE issues and the preparation for work placement.

This case study offered an opportunity to review how effectively students were being prepared for employment, and to monitor their understanding of key dimensions of employability. According to Yorke and Knight (2006) there is no 'one size fits all' approach to embedding employability in the curriculum. Educators have an opportunity to embed employability through the whole curriculum, within core modules, through work-based or work-related learning or employability related modules within the curriculum (Yorke and Knight, 2006). Yorke and Knight (2006: 17) observe there appears to be a 'growing emphasis on the development of students' skills at the beginning of their programmes of study, centring on freestanding "skills" modules of varying kinds'. After a brief discussion with the programme leaders, it was decided to embed employability development into a compulsory first year module called *Understanding Hospitality Businesses*.

The module

Yorke and Knight would define the *Understanding Hospitality Businesses* module as an 'employability-related module' designed to support the development of students' employability skills in their first year of study. The module aims to deliver 'subject understanding', 'skilful practices' and 'personal qualities' in terms of the USEM model presented by Yorke and Knight (2006: 5). Students are introduced also in the first year to the concept of reflective practice and 'metacognition', but this is more focused on in another compulsory module elsewhere in the curriculum.

Figure 1 The USEM model of Yorke and Knight (2006)

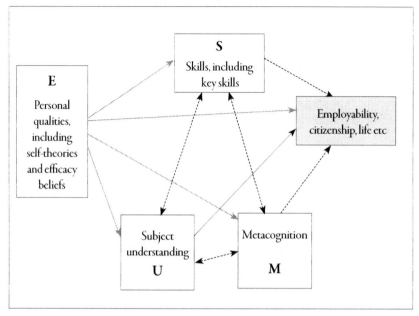

Source: Yorke, M. and Knight, P. T. (2006) *Embedding employability into the curriculum*. Learning and Employability Series One. York: HEA Enhancing Student Employability Co-ordination Team

A key question at the outset of the case study was how to measure impact on students' learning and also on their development of skills. The level of complexity inevitably impacts on the question of how to measure employability. Certain aspects of assessment could measure students' ability to construct an effective CV and LTA activities could focus on developing job-seeking skills such as job applications and interviewing. It was decided it may be useful to try and ascertain what impact the module had on students' perceptions of the importance of employability skills by using the '39 attributes' suggested by Yorke and Knight (2006: 8). Although a questionnaire is a crude tool for measuring complex understandings and can only give data on perceptions, it was felt that it could be a useful gauge of how well the module had impacted upon students' thinking surrounding employability.

Description

The module used as the focus for this case study had already been running successfully for a number of years. However, it was felt by the module team that employability skills development could be made a more explicit part of the module. It had become apparent that students going on work placement in year 2 generally had a poor understanding of the skills required by employers and the types of job oppor-

Figure 2 *Understanding Hospitality Businesses* **module overview**

Outline of weekly activities

Week	Lecture	Seminar activities
1	Concepts of hospitality and industry structure	Introduction to module / Study skills – group work
2	Characteristics of service and hospitality Employability Skills Questionnaire 1	Study skills – presentations & essays
3	Customer expectations and quality	Debate – the nature of hospitality
4	Standardisation	Mini-presentation – sectors
5	Essay writing and academic integrity	Presentation – customer expectations by sector
6	Employment	Writing skills & feedback
7	CV Preparation	Debate – uniqueness
8	Interpersonal skills	Employer's needs exercise **Deadline: Essay due Friday 10am**
9	Diversity	Evaluating CVs
10	Industry Issues Overview	Interviewing practice **Deadline: Final CV due Thursday 10am**
11	Reading week	Industry issues discussion / exam preparation Employability Skills Questionnaire 2
12	No lecture	In-class test Module feedback forms

Outcome:
An employable student who understands the wider context of the hospitality industry

tunities available in the industry. The CVs produced by students were also generally considered to be below standard. The intervention therefore focused on raising students' awareness of the importance of employability, their knowledge of the labour market and the skills required by employers in different industry sectors, and their job application skills (e.g. CV writing). After some research in the area there were a number of new activities introduced into the module in 2005–06, including:

❑ an employability card-sort exercise

❑ an analysis of employment characteristics in different sectors of hospitality and tourism

❑ an evaluation of employer needs via analysis of job adverts
❑ a CV lecture and CV-writing workshop, with peer review
❑ introduction of a mock interview, with peer review.

Before evaluating some of these activities in greater detail it may be useful to present an overview of the module and how these activities fitted in with the overall study programme, see Figure 2.

An extract from the module handbook explains Figure 2 and the aims of the module:

The triangle indicates the narrowing of the content from broad definitions and the scope and nature of the industry through operational aspects to questions of employment and employability. The objectives of the course are thus to provide an introduction to:

a   the scope and characteristics of the industry;

b   some of the conceptual frameworks that are used to analyse it;

c   customer behaviour and expectations;

d   management issues in meeting those expectations;

e   the role of employees in that process;

f   how you can best prepare yourself to be an employee in the industry;

g   academic skills necessary to be successful at the university.

This module is part of vocational courses in hospitality and tourism. As noted above, its aim is to help you to become more employable, particularly in preparing you for obtaining jobs in your placement year. Interviews for that placement will take place in semester 2 of this year.

Employability is closely linked to the learning objectives of the module, in terms of:

a   your knowledge of the industry and its management;

b   transferable skills, (team work, analysing information, writing, presenting, etc.);

c   job seeking skills (understanding employers' needs, preparation of CVs, interviewing skills).

You are encouraged to see all the work on the module in this light and recognise that all three aspects contribute to your ability to persuade an employer to hire you, for your placement, for part-time work or for a job after graduation.

(Extract from module handbook 2006–07)

The diagram and short narrative is intended to make students and tutors aware from the outset that employability is one of the key outcomes of the module, and how it is structured to achieve this. The tutor handbook also contains specific references to employability so that tutors can make explicit reference to this in relation to the weekly teaching and learning activities.

Employability card-sort

The card-sort exercise is designed to stimulate thought processes about what employability is and to help students better understand the skills/attributes required for successful employment. This exercise takes place in a tutor-led workshop in week 8 of the semester. Early reference to card-sorts was made by Tyler (1961) when he introduced an occupational card-sort drawing on personal construct theory in vocational counselling. Hopson and Scally (1984) introduced self-reflective card-sorts into the UK at the University of Leeds where they were used by the Centre for Counselling and Career Development Unit (CCDU) for self-reflection on interests, skills and values. Card-sorts have since been used in many aspects of teaching and the card-sort developed at Oxford Brookes, which is based on the work of ESECT, has three stages:

❑ 'Employability is ...' encourages individuals (by using examples) to articulate their views on what 'employability' might mean, discuss these views with colleagues and modify them if appropriate (stage 1).

❑ 'Employability outcomes' stimulates clear thinking of what employability attributes a practitioner may wish to develop in his/her students through their academic experiences (stage 2).

❑ 'Techniques' raises awareness of a wide range of techniques and learning approaches currently practised which may be used to achieve the desired employability outcomes (stage 3).

The card sort is an extremely useful teaching resource that can be used to raise awareness of employability, and also to help students (and teachers) plan for employability development. For much more detailed information on this card sort and to download the cards see the Higher Education Academy website at: http://www. heacademy.ac.uk/resources/detail/id459_card_sorts_in_employability_learning

Sheffield Hallam University CETL (e3i) also have developed a card sort that can be used by other HE providers. See their website at http://extra.shu.ac.uk/cetl/e3iresources.html

Evaluation of job adverts

This activity is designed to get students thinking about what employers are looking for in potential employees. Students scrutinise a range of quite detailed job adverts for hospitality and tourism jobs and undertake the following activity:

1   Identify the key attributes required in this job.

2   Analyse these into the categories shown on the form we have provided you with

and organise the attributes under personal characteristics, academic qualifications, and prior experience.

3   Compare the five adverts in your analysis and analyse similarities/differences in terms of attributes sought and the level of job, the sector it relates to, locations and so on.

4   Write down what the advert seems to say about the organisation and its culture.

5   Write down if this is an attractive company to work for and why.

This discussion after the activity was very useful in getting students to really think about the skills employers are looking for and how this might link to their own skills development.

CV and mock interview

These activities are designed to focus much more on developing students' skills in CV writing and interviewing. They are asked to peer-review another student's CV for a particular placement job and the following week to interview them for that role. The student is required to think in more depth about the skills/attributes the employer is seeking and to structure questions in a way that try to ascertain if the individual has those skills. This focuses students' minds on the types of questions they might be asked at interview and how they themselves would evidence particular skills to an employer. In 2006–07 it was decided to formally assess the CV as part of the module awarding it a few marks (5% of overall total). This served to increase students' awareness of the importance of producing a good CV and staff in the Careers & Work Experience Office in the department noticed a marked improvement in the students' CVs over the previous years.

Evaluation

A key part of this case study was to examine the changes in students' perceptions of the importance of a range of employability skills over the period of the module. The questionnaire used was based around the 39 attributes of employability produced by Yorke and Knight (2006: 8). It should be recognised that this is not a direct measure of the students' employability, though it could be argued that an increased awareness is an increase in their knowledge of what is important in getting a job. The questionnaire was administered at the beginning and end of the module for two cohorts of students (2005–06 and 2006–07) and the results are presented below.

The results showed some significant changes in perceptions over the three months between questionnaires. It needs to be recognised that the module does not take place in a vacuum. Students are involved in other modules (not always the same ones) and many will have done part-time work for the first time. These will inevitably have an influence on their perceptions of employability and the questionnaire cannot hope to establish direct cause and effect. However it does offer some useful insights into students' perceptions.

a   The most significant changes were in the area of job-seeking skills. Typically the change was between 15–25% typically from a fairly low base of 50–60%, suggesting limited perceptions at the outset of the importance of this aspect of employability.

b   Discipline knowledge still remains as the dominant feature of students' perceptions of what is important to employability. Typically students rated this aspect much higher (85–95%) in the first questionnaire and these levels were maintained or slightly increased over the period.

c   There was a notable increase in awareness of 'soft' skills such as self-management, listening, written communication and oral presentations. Interestingly there was little change in topics not part of the module such as numeracy and a decrease of 8% in language skills.

d   Personal qualities such as self-awareness, self confidence and independence showed little change over the semester.

Detailed figures and evaluation of questionnaire results

Table 1   Factors influencing success in career (ranked as very important/important)

Importance of:	Pre-intervention Survey		Post-intervention Survey		Change from Pre to Post	
	2005–06	2006–07	2005–06	2006–07	2005–06	2006–07
Chance	36%	37%	35%	53%	- 1%	16%
Level of education	64%	69%	65%	62%	1%	-7%
Political influence	21%	24%	15%	16%	6%	-8%
Personal achievement	79%	82%	74%	83%	-7%	1%
Ruthlessness	40%	28%	34%	35%	6%	7%
Honesty	67%	61%	58%	69%	9%	8%
Connections	71%	70%	64%	77%	-7%	7%
Initiative	80%	83%	77%	77%	-3%	-6%

Some interesting results which show that students ranked initiative, connections and personal achievement highly at both start and end of the module. Level of education and honesty also rank highly. It is interesting to note the increase (16%) in students from the 2006–07 cohort ranking 'chance' as important, although without further qualitative analysis it is not clear why more than 50% of the cohort thought this at the end of the module.

Table 2   Personal qualities ranked as very important/quite important

Personal qualities	Pre-intervention Survey		Post-intervention Survey		Change from Pre to Post	
Importance of:	2005–06	2006–07	2005–06	2006–07	2005–06	2006–07
Willingness to learn	86%	84%	91%	92%	5%	7%
Adaptability	94%	86%	91%	91%	3%	5%
Reflectiveness	72%	64%	74%	71%	2%	7%
Malleable self theory	75%	67%	78%	74%	3%	7%

These are encouraging signs of students' increasing awareness of the need to reflect, learn and change. It is also encouraging to note that categories such as self awareness, self confidence and independence, which consistently rated around 90% plus. Emotional intelligence, reflectiveness and malleable self theory scored in the 70s. Although the module does not focus on development of personal qualities *per se* it would be nice to think that the teaching and learning experience on the module encouraged the improvements in rankings.

Table 3   Core skills ranked as very important/quite important

Core Skills	Pre-intervention Survey		Post-intervention Survey		Change from Pre to Post	
Importance of:	2005–06	2006–07	2005–06	2006–07	2005–06	2006–07
Information retrieval	71%	58%	71%	65%	0%	7%
Language skills	67%	54%	60%	58%	-7%	4%
Self-management	87%	84%	93%	90%	6%	6%
Creativity	80%	71%	82%	85%	2%	14%
Listening	80%	76%	87%	85%	6%	9%
Global awareness	79%	73%	76%	83%	-3%	10%

Self-management and listening are ranked as important by the majority of students and increases in the former may be a result of the fact that at university students are expected to manage themselves/their learning more than they might at school. Listening is also emphasised in the card-sort and interviewing-skills workshops delivered on the module. Language skills were the lowest-ranking core skills cited by students, and maybe this is because most are targeting English-speaking countries for their placement. Another point to note is that most core skills were perceived as more important at the end of the module, suggesting that maybe the student teaching and learning experiences had influenced students' perceptions in these areas.

Table 4 Process skills ranked as very important/quite important

Importance of:	Pre-intervention Survey		Post-intervention Survey		Change from Pre to Post	
	2005–06	2006–07	2005–06	2006–07	2005–06	2006–07
Prioritising	84%	78%	77%	78%	-7%	0%
Arguing for / justifying	75%	75%	80%	68%	5%	-7%
Ethical sensitivity	80%	69%	76%	76%	-4%	7%
Decision making	85%	86%	92%	89%	7%	3%

The fall in importance for 'prioritising' in 2005 was surprising in that the module introduced students to a range of activities and deadlines where they had to decide what work to do and in what order. It did not repeat itself in 2006 though both ended at the same level. 'Decision making' showed a consistently high result in each year. The slight percentage point decrease in 'Arguing for/justifying' in 2006/7 is difficult to understand given the need to argue and make decisions in the presentations, essays and even in seminar discussions where students have to analyse and evaluate situations relating to the industry and come to conclusions and recommendations for action.

Table 5 Job Search Skills ranked as very important/quite important

Importance of:	Pre-intervention Survey		Post-intervention Survey		Change from Pre to Post	
	2005–06	2006–07	2005–06	2006–07	2005–06	2006–07
Knowledge of types of jobs available	43%	35%	55%	52%	12%	17%
Know skills employers think important	46%	44%	68%	57%	22%	13%
Know where to look for jobs I want	23%	19%	29%	30%	6%	11%
How to write a good CV	30%	31%	57%	59%	**27%**	**28%**
Confidence filling out application forms	35%	29%	45%	50%	10%	21%
Confidence in talking to employers	48%	48%	61%	63%	13%	15%
Know what job I want in future	49%	52%	51%	64%	2%	12%
Know who in University can advise	36%	26%	46%	54%	10%	28%

The increase in importance from beginning to end of module in CV writing is particularly marked for both cohorts of students. In general looking at the results in Table 5, it would be reasonable to conclude that students believed they had greatly improved their job hunting skills and this is a result of the embedding of specific related activities in the module. However it is still rather worrying that only 59% of students think knowledge of how to write a good CV is important to their career and less than a third of students think 'know where to look for jobs I want' is important. In comparison with the employability attributes, the job search skills ranked as less important overall which may need to be addressed in future runs of the module.

Discussion
Enablers that helped practice to work

1   Having a clear strategy on the shape of the module and the relationship to employability.
2   Explicit information to tutors at each stage of the module on how the teaching and learning methods on the module are intended to influence employability.
3   Linking theoretical concepts to practical activities to demonstrate the importance of developing both conceptual and practical aspects of employability.

Points of advice

1   Think carefully about the questionnaire design. Questionnaires are often most effective when kept as short and as focused as possible and the one used in this case study was rather lengthy.
2   Interpretation of the quantitative results would be strengthened by a follow-up with qualitative research (e.g. interviews or focus groups) on questions that cannot be fully understood on a quantitative basis. The quantitative results say what the change was but it is difficult, if not impossible, to determine why the change might have occurred without asking students more searching questions.
3   It would be helpful if follow-up interviews or focus groups could be held both before (but soon after the second questionnaire) and after the interviews for their placements. The former might help to understand the reasons for the changes in the quantitative results while the latter would enable students to discuss how they had benefited from the module post-placement.
4   It is necessary to recognise the limitations in the existing knowledge and vocabulary of students. Some concepts that are common in research or pedagogic literature may not mean as much to them, particularly first year students, as they do to the researcher.

Benefits to end-users

Perceived benefits	
For students...	**For staff...**
Increased awareness of the management skills as factors influencing employability Increased awareness of the importance of specific employability skills Increased knowledge of importance of job-search skills	Improved understanding of employability and how to embed aspects of development in the curriculum Increased focus on employability as an underlying factor in module design and delivery Integration of a wide range of theory and practical work aimed at improving the employability of students Increased understanding of students' perception of employability Increased understanding of the nature and importance of employability
Issues/Challenges	
For students...	**For staff...**
Recognising the relationship between what is taught in the classroom and the practical aspects of employability Understanding employers' expectations and what they can do to meet them Mixing theoretical and practical activities Getting students to understand the importance of job search skills	Recognising the challenges facing students, particularly their lack of awareness of the importance of personal, transferable and job-seeking skills. Adjusting teaching methods to demonstrate the theoretical underpinning of practical skills development Planning in time for staff training to provide guidance on using the card-sort and other tools

5 Analyse and evaluate the results as soon after administering the questionnaire as possible, documenting the thinking behind it in as much detail as possible. This is particularly helpful when working on later years results when recall can be difficult.

6 Build in a feedback process from tutors on various aspects of employability so that their input can inform the interpretation of student results. Tutors should be encouraged to ask for qualitative feedback from students in the seminars.

Possible improvements

The following changes would appear to be desirable following this research:

1 It is important that the questionnaire is tailored to the needs and context of the

participant group.

2   The employability agenda could be articulated even more clearly to students and tutors, through handbooks, guidance notes and in lectures/seminars.

3   The use of the current questionnaire provided primarily quantitative results. It would be helpful to arrange focus groups, preferably after the students have been through their placement, to obtain a qualitative insight into how perceptions had changed and the students' views on the module/their employability after working for a year.

Further comments

The study should have relevance to many other HE institutions faced with the issues of transition from school to higher education and, if Knight and Yorke (2006) are correct, with the need to build employability and new formative assessment measures into first-year modules rather than leave them until later. The case study approach and module activities would be relatively easy and inexpensive to administer in other HE courses. The questionnaire utilitised did provide valuable information about changes in student perceptions of employability and although not directly measuring employability itself, the results can be used to inform curriculum development and ways of embedding employability into an academic module.

Reading/Resources

Dearing, R. (1997) *The Dearing Report – National Committee of Inquiry into Higher Education. National Report – Future demands for higher education*

HEFCE (2001) Performance indicators in higher education: 1998–99, 1999–2000. Bristol: Higher Education Funding Council for England (HEA)

Hopson, B. and Scally, M. (1984) *Build Your Own Rainbow: A Workbook for Career and Life Management*. Leeds: Lifeskills Publishing Group

Knight, P. T. and Yorke, M. (2006) Employability: judging and communicating achievements. *Learning and Employability Series One*. York: HEA – Enhancing Student Employability Co-ordination Team.

Lees, D. (2002) *Information for Academic Staff on Employability*. LTSN Generic Centre

Tyler, L. E. (1961) Research Exploration in the Realm of Choice. *Journal of Counseling Psychology* 8 pp. 195–202

Yorke, M. (2006) Employability and higher education: what it is – what it is not. *Learning and Employability Series One*. York: HEA – Enhancing Student Employability Co-ordination Team

Yorke, M. and Knight, P. T. (2006) Embedding employability into the curriculum. *Learning and Employability Series One*. York: HEA – Enhancing Student Employability Co-ordination Team

Glossary

CeAL	Centre of Excellence in Active Learning	HRM	human resource management
CCDU	Counselling and Career Development Unit	HTL	hospitality, tourism and leisure
CCN	City College Norwich	ICT	information and communications technology
CDT	course development team		
CETL	Centre for Excellence in Teaching and Learning	IEEP	International Entrepreneurship Educators Programme
CIEH	Chartered Institute of Environmental Health	IHM	International Hospitality Management
CIPD	Chartered Institute of Personnel and Development	IHTM	International Hospitality and Tourism Management
CPD	Continuing Professional Development	IMI	Intrinsic Motivation Inventory questionnaire
DDA	Disability Discrimination Act 2005	LJMU	Liverpool John Moores University
DIS	Diploma in Industrial Studies (UU)	LTA	learning, teaching and assessment
DIUS	Department for Innovation, Universities and Skills	M&B	Mitchells and Butlers
		NCGE	National Council for Graduate Entrepreneurship
DSCF	Department for Schools, Children and Families		
		PDP	personal development planning
DFES	Department for Education and Skills	PDS	Personal Development System (UU)
DfEE	Department for Education and Employment	PE	physical education
		PG	postgraduate
DIUS	Department for Innovation, Universities and Skills	POM	*Principles of Management*
		QAA	Quality Assurance Agency
e3i	Sheffield Hallam University CETL	SES	Self-Esteem Scale (Rosenberg, 1989)
ECI-U	Emotional Competence Inventory	SHU	Sheffield Hallam University
ELLI	Effective Lifelong Learning Inventory	SME	small and medium-sized enterprise
ERASMUS	European Community Action Scheme for the Mobility of University Students	SPEED	a national student business competition
		SWE	supervised work experience
		SWOT	strengths, weaknesses, opportunities, threats analysis
ERZ	Employability Resource Zone		
ESECT	Enhancing Student Employability Co-ordination Team	TE3	Technology Enhanced Enterprise Education fund
FdAs	Foundation degrees in Arts	TIFF	Temple Index of Functional Fluency
fdf	Foundation Degree Forward	TLA	teaching, learning and assessment
FDTL	Fund for the Development of Teaching and Learning	UCLan	University of Central Lancashire
		UoW	University of Worcester
HEFCE	Higher Education Funding Council for England	USEM	Understanding of subject matter, Skilful practices, Efficacy beliefs and Meta-cognition model cf. Yorke and Knight (2006)
HEA	HE Academy *also* HE Authority (N Ireland)		
		UU	University of Ulster
HEI	Higher Education Institution	WBA	work-based assessment
HLST	hospitality, leisure, sport and tourism *also* HE Academy Subject Network for Hospitality, Leisure, Sport and Tourism	WBL	work-based learning
		WebCT	a virtual-learning environment (VLE)
		WRA	work-related assessment
HND	Higher National Diploma	WRL	work-related learning

Index